BROMBERG BROS.

BLUE
RIBBON

COOKBOOK

BROMBERG BROS.
BLUE RIBBON COOKBOOK

Better Home Cooking

BRUCE BROMBERG | ERIC BROMBERG

AND MELISSA CLARK

PHOTOGRAPHS BY QUENTIN BACON

CLARKSON POTTER/PUBLISHERS
NEW YORK

To Robert and Bruno, for your teachings and dedication. You have shown us what matters, not only in the kitchen, but, more important, in life.

To Grandma Martha, Mom, and Dad. You have nourished us not just with food, but with love, support, and encouragement.

It is from all of your inspiration that Blue Ribbon was born.

Copyright © 2010 by Eric Bromberg and Bruce Bromberg
Photographs copyright © 2010 by Quentin Bacon

Published in the United States by Clarkson Potter/
Publishers, an imprint of the Crown Publishing Group,
a division of Random House, Inc., New York.
www.crownpublishing.com
www.clarksonpotter.com

CLARKSON POTTER is a trademark and POTTER
with colophon is a registered trademark of Random
House, Inc.

Library of Congress Cataloging-in-Publication Data is
available upon request.

ISBN 978-0-307-40794-8

Printed in China

Design by Stephanie Huntwork

10 9 8 7 6 5 4 3 2 1

First Edition

contents

introduction

As brothers, we have always been close, always at each other's side, always on the same team. The only time we were actually competitors was at summer camp when we used to try to outdo each other at waterskiing. When the prizes were handed out the only thing either of us wanted to take home was the first-place ribbons; we still keep them tacked up in our bedrooms at our mom's house. The blue ribbon, signifying victory and unquestioned excellence, and incidentally the name of our alma mater Le Cordon Bleu, was the only thing worth fighting for. In 1992, when we unexpectedly won the lease to our dream property at 97 Sullivan Street, in the SoHo neighborhood of New York City, we knew there could be only one name for our restaurant: Blue Ribbon.

But coming up with a name for your dream restaurant and actually opening said restaurant are two entirely different things. There was a sobering amount of work to be done to get Blue Ribbon up and running, and we had next to no funds available to accomplish the task. Wielding sledgehammers, we gutted the premises of 97 Sullivan—an emotional process considering that the former tenant was the Crystal Room, our opulent classical French restaurant that was the offshoot of SoHo's beloved Nick and Eddie. We couldn't have done it without a lot of help from our ever-loyal crew, who are still with us today. Our friends pitched in with no thought of compensation—Kris Polak, Sean Sant Amour, David Brown, Michael Paritsky, Morgan Grove, Scott Henkle, Francisco Palaquibay, Jim Shrum, and Alonso Almeida (we've worked with Shrum and Almeida since our time at the American Hotel at Sag Harbor back in the '80s). Even Suzanne Allgair, our childhood friend and Bruce's cooking school class-mate, took time off from her paying gig in Telluride to help us paint. We made constant trips to Metropolitan Lumber on Spring Street for building materials (and for advice on what to do with all the stuff we were buying). We found an electrician who agreed to defer his fee until we opened (in part because of a prior electrical mishap that had left Eric unconscious and the electrician feeling guilty), and we had a plumber (programmed on speed dial) who patiently explained how to wrangle the errant pipes and who would occasionally lend us his tools. We installed everything from the Sheetrock to the kitchen sink ourselves. Somehow, and no one was more amazed than we were (though we tried not to show it), we were ready to open on November 3, 1992. We triumphantly scheduled a party for one of our investors who had stuck with us through those crazy months, and we worked on the place up until the last moment—when we noticed the guests had arrived but were just standing around outside looking confused. That's when it hit us: we hadn't yet put in the door handles. A few turns of the screwdriver and Blue Ribbon opened its doors.

Even though we had no other choice than to go the do-it-yourself route, finances being what they were, it turned out to be the best possible way for us to start our business. For one thing, it led to our policy of staying open from four P.M. to four A.M. Working on a deadline as we were—knowing every day we weren't open was costing us money we didn't have—we worked at renovating the restaurant around the clock. We often didn't have a chance to eat until the dead of night and soon made a discovery: this may be the city that never sleeps, but it sure wasn't eating anything good after midnight. There were a handful of places open at that hour and their menus seemed to be limited to only the dishes their prep cooks could put together. After a summer spent eating a ton of overcooked steaks and uninspired salads, we decided that late-night dining was a niche Blue Ribbon was meant to fill. Of course, it took a while before our idea caught on. In the early days, after about eleven P.M. the restaurant would empty out and we'd either hold rock-and-roll jam sessions in the basement or come up with new dishes just to keep ourselves busy. But we knew we had to stick with it; we did, and the market found us.

In addition to keeping an unheard-of operating schedule, Blue Ribbon employed a nontraditional reservation policy. We didn't take them. This was a brilliant innovation that Eric's wife, Ellen, came up with when she was acting as the hostess at Nick and Eddie while Eric was the chef. Ellen had a firsthand view of customers' frustration waiting hours for a table when there were unoccupied seats in plain view. The no-reservation policy is a much more democratic way to seat people: if there is a table open, whoever gets there first gets it. Nowadays, it's industry standard, but back then it was considered a crazy idea that no one thought would work.

Before long we became known as the after-hours place for chefs, cooks, waiters, bartenders, and the like—mostly thanks to Drew Nieporent, who single-handedly informed the entire restaurant community that we were a real restaurant that stayed open after midnight. Restaurant folks make the best customers, and we loved having Mario Batali, Bobby Flay, Tom Colicchio, Daniel Boulud, Jean-Georges Vongerichten, and our old pal Billy Gillroy from Lucky Strike sit at our tables or take a stool at our bar. We bounced ideas off each other and tasted each other's latest recipes— Mario would bring over that night's crostini creation, Daniel would pass around foie gras, and we would send Sean down to Chinatown just before service to pick up live crabs that we'd steam for everybody. We were cooking in ways we never would have thought of if it hadn't been for that exuberant back-and-forth between chefs; it was an environment in which everybody thrived.

As for the food on the menu, while some of it is exactly what our instructors at Le Cordon Bleu taught us to make, much of it veers off into another direction completely.

We serve the food we love—food we feel a real passion for. And just as we turned into DIYers to create the restaurant's physical space, no element of our menu is too humble or inconsequential for us to create from scratch. We started making our own pickles and pickled peppers, hamburger buns and french fries, hot fudge and hot sauce, and we even import our own brand of Blue Ribbon honey from Mexico. It's all about valuing each step of the process (something instilled in us in France). No matter what dish we're working on, our aim is to elevate it to its highest expression while still remaining true to its nature. If fried chicken was going to find a place on our menu, it had to be the finest fried chicken possible. As a result, the Blue Ribbon kitchen has made interpretations of classic French recipes, Chinatown-inspired fare, and dishes (some of our most popular ones) straight from the New Jersey diners we grew up eating in. What's good is good; there's no food snobbery here.

We like to think of our menu as a meritocracy, where each dish has proven itself first with our restaurant team, and then with our customers. We've been thrilled by the response we've received from our patrons. The success of the first Blue Ribbon that opened in 1992 has allowed us to branch out with Blue Ribbon Sushi, Blue Ribbon Bakery, and restaurant locations in Midtown and Brooklyn. Each outpost has its own style, dictated by the neighborhood's clientele and the setup of the kitchen. For example, Blue Ribbon Sushi's kitchen is minuscule with room for only a couple of hot plates, which has led to the creation of some dainty dishes; the brick oven in the basement of the Bakery has allowed us to experiment with roasting huge joints of meat and to try out some fantastic bread recipes. Trial and error (and some brilliant inspirations) have led us to unique menus for each of our nine New York City locations.

Blue Ribbon all started with that crazy summer of construction on Sullivan Street, but it took years and years of hard work to get to that point. We brothers Bromberg have worked, together and separately, in restaurants from Paris, France, to Boulder, Colorado, and many points in between. We've picked up more than a few bits of wisdom along the way: how to perfectly poach an egg (page 193), how to save a broken sauce (page 239), how to get truly creamy crème brûlée (page 147), and many, many more. When we were able to team up and create our own restaurants, our guiding principle was experimentation. We rarely regard a dish as "finished." Before it ever makes it out of the kitchen, it has been tested and retested by us or by a crew member, or even, as in the case of Spicy Egg Shooters (page 21) and the Stanwich (page 188), by customers or family members. Many times a dish starts out as a kitchen snack before going through a series of improvements until we finally realize it would be selfish not to put it on the menu.

We've found the inspiration for our dishes from the kitchens of our Parisian apprenticeships (Beef Marrow Bones with Oxtail Marmalade, page 84, and Crunchy Potato Cakes, page 123); from the culinary tourism that Dad used to force on us as kids—thanks, Dad!—(Grilled and Marinated Crudités, page 69, and Shrimp Provençal with Pernod, page 107); from old family recipes (Martha's Excellent Matzoh Ball Soup, page 64, and Really Good Brisket, page 90); and from our favorite Jersey eateries (Homemade Challah Bread, page 200, and Mom's Egg Salad Sandwich, page 208). Some dishes have no clear provenance; they are born from a mix of necessity and stubbornness, because if somebody tells us something can't be done, well, that's exactly what we need to hear to spur us on to accomplishment (Northern Fried Chicken, page 98, and Banana Walnut Bread Pudding with Butterscotch-Banana Sauce, page 151).

We've arranged the chapters in the book to follow the schedule we've kept for years as chefs. That's why we start out with Nibbles, Snacks, and Toasts—because, especially back in the days when we first opened the restaurant, that 4:00 P.M. meal was the one we'd usually have to begin our busy workday. Appetizers, Soups, and Salads is next, followed by the Main Dishes, Vegetables and Sides, and Desserts (which we'd sit down to around 12:30 A.M., Blue Ribbon's traditional lull). Breakfast and Brunch is our sociable meal at home with our families. And Sandwiches? We have offerings to suit every time of day or night. But feel free to read the chapters in any order. Maybe you like to start your day with dessert? It's a free country.

We've chosen to share the recipes for Blue Ribbon's most-loved dishes—ones that are as "finished" as they're going to get. We've retested, tweaked, and polished them up with instructions and tips meant for the home cook. Hopefully they'll motivate you to conduct some culinary experiments of your own. And who knows? Maybe you'll drop by the restaurant, have a drink at the bar, and tell us what new twists you came up with or let us in on some of your family's culinary secrets. In our experience, there's nothing like a little friendly back-and-forth to inspire a wonderful meal; that's what Blue Ribbon is all about.

nibbles, snacks, and toasts

◙ trio of spreads: beet, olive, and anchovy with flatbread

◙ cumin-roasted almonds ◙ spicy egg shooters ◙ spicy cheese crackers ◙ roasted tomato, arugula, and lemon toasts ◙ stilton toasts with honey-port glaze ◙ whole roasted garlic with warm country bread toasts

◙ manchego and mexican honey toasts ◙ pork rillettes and cornichon toasts ◙ goat cheese toasts with grilled red onion and roasted tomato ◙ duck confit and dijon mustard toasts

◙ country pâté and shallot confit toasts

◙ arugula, red pepper, and goat cheese flatbread

◙ bacon and red onion flatbread ◙ matzoh

We have always enjoyed little bites at Blue Ribbon. There's an appealing sense of abundance when you get your food in easy-to-sample sizes and can taste lots of different dishes at once. And really, you could make a full meal out of a combination of any three or four of these recipes.

Tiny bites to enjoy between meals—or with a glass of wine as a prelude to dinner—all have one thing in common: lots and lots of flavor. When you're serving up just a mouthful or two, there's no need to pull any punches. Break out the fancy cheese: you'll only need a little bit to spread on piping-hot toast, so you might as well reach for that precious wedge of Stilton. Add a drizzle of good Mexican honey and you'll be in snack nirvana in no time. The best bites are simple to make and go down easy; sometimes we can barely get the snack out of the kitchen, they're so tempting to gobble up.

Some of these we developed on the fly because we needed something to munch on the double or because we had a surplus of a certain ingredient that needed to be put to use (Cumin-Roasted Almonds, page 19, and Whole Roasted Garlic with Warm Country Bread Toasts, page 28), and then ended up serving them for years and years because people loved them so much. Others, such as Trio of Spreads: Beet, Olive, and Anchovy with Flatbread (page 16) and Matzoh (page 41) were the snacks claimed as a "chef's privilege"—little treats we ate with gusto in the kitchen for ages before we realized that they were something that ought to be placed on the menu.

Whatever you choose to make, mix and match for ultimate satisfaction, and in no time you'll be coming up with your own delectable combinations.

TRIO OF SPREADS
BEET, OLIVE, AND ANCHOVY WITH FLATBREAD

MAKES ABOUT 1 CUP OF EACH SPREAD; SERVES 12 TO 16

The three spreads on this plate were all originally created either as condiments or as building blocks for other dishes. We use the anchovy spread for our Caesar salad and the beet and olive spreads for sandwiches. But in the kitchen we would find ourselves smearing them on flatbread or matzoh as impromptu snacks. They are all very addictive in their own way—the sweet, intense beets; the salty, meaty olives; the briny anchovies. Anyway, this snacking went on for some time before it dawned on us that each of these spreads has value in its own right and that we really should share all three with our customers.

BEET SPREAD

3 medium beets, scrubbed and trimmed

2 tablespoons olive oil

1 large red onion, peeled and thickly sliced

½ cup Roasted Red Peppers (page 231)

Kosher salt and freshly ground black pepper

OLIVE SPREAD

3 cups pitted kalamata olives, juice reserved

½ cup drained brine-packed capers

¾ cup Roasted Red Peppers (page 231)

½ cup extra-virgin olive oil

ANCHOVY SPREAD

6 tablespoons drained brine-packed anchovies

2 tablespoons drained brine-packed capers

1 garlic clove, minced

½ cup extra-virgin olive oil

¾ teaspoon freshly squeezed lemon juice

Flatbread (see pages 38 and 40), Matzoh (page 41), or other bread and/or crackers, for serving

1 TO MAKE THE BEET SPREAD: Preheat the oven to 350°F.

2 Place the beets in a roasting pan, toss with 1 tablespoon of the oil, and add 2 tablespoons water to the bottom of the pan. Cover with foil and roast until very tender, 1 to 1½ hours. Let cool then peel and coarsely chop.

recipe continues

3   Preheat a grill, grill pan, or broiler. Brush the onion slices with the remaining tablespoon oil and grill or broil, turning once, until golden brown and soft, about 7 minutes. Let cool, then coarsely chop.

4   In a food processor, combine 1 cup of the beets, ½ cup of the onion, and the red peppers (reserve leftover beets and onions for another purpose). Process until finely chopped. Scrape into a bowl.

5   TO MAKE THE OLIVE SPREAD: In a food processor, combine the olives, capers, and red peppers. Process until finely chopped. Add the olive oil and pulse until smooth, drizzling in the reserved olive juice through the feeder tube until a spreadable consistency is reached.

6   TO MAKE THE ANCHOVY SPREAD: In a food processor, combine the anchovies, capers, and garlic. Process until finely chopped. Add the olive oil and lemon juice and process until smooth, about 5 minutes.

7   Serve the spreads in little bowls with the flatbread.

CUMIN-ROASTED ALMONDS

MAKES ABOUT 3 CUPS

Eric came up with this one at the American Hotel in Sag Harbor, New York. He started there as a salad chef, and because of a succession of chefs quitting, he ended up becoming *chef de cuisine* about two months later—the fastest promotion ever. That was 1986, the year the Mets made their World Series run, and for that week, there was always a crowd at the bar to watch the games. One particular night, the hotel's patriarch, Ted Conklin, rushed into the kitchen saying, "Everybody wants snacks—do what you can do!" Eager to please, Eric poked around the pantry and came up with a five-pound can of almonds, some cumin, kosher salt, and a jug of peanut oil, which he just tossed all together and baked. Minutes later, Mookie was rounding first, Buckner hung his head in shame, Ray Knight leapt toward home, and the Mets and these tasty snacks were destined for glory. Oh, what a night!

When we put these on the menu at Blue Ribbon, we originally used blanched almonds, but once we tried making them with the un-skinned almonds we never went back. The skins add so much flavor. But really, this recipe works with any kind of raw nut, skins on or off.

1 pound raw, unpeeled almonds

3 tablespoons canola oil

3 tablespoons extra-virgin olive oil

1½ tablespoons kosher salt, more if needed

2¼ teaspoons ground cumin

1　Preheat the oven to 350°F.

2　In a large bowl, toss the almonds, canola oil, olive oil, salt, and cumin together and mix well. Spread in a single layer on a rimmed baking sheet. Roast, stirring once halfway through, until golden, 20 to 25 minutes.

3　Transfer the pan to a wire rack to cool slightly. Sprinkle with more salt, if desired, while still warm. Serve warm or at room temperature. The almonds can be kept in an airtight container at room temperature for up to 1 week.

SPICY EGG SHOOTERS

We started making these hard-boiled-egg snacks when we were building and opening Blue Ribbon Bakery. One day, a farmer from upstate showed up at our door. He explained that he had only a handful of birds and produced a modest number of eggs per week, but he was sure if we tried the eggs we'd be hooked.

We put a pot of water on the stove, and in went several of the randomly sized and colored day-old eggs. Once they were boiled and we sliced them in half, the yolks were vibrant and the whites pristine and pale. The eggs tasted fantastic all by themselves, but when Flavio Guaman, our sous-chef, sliced up a jalapeño to put on top, sprinkled on some kosher salt, and gave one to the farmer, it was the farmer's turn for revelation! We added a little mayo and decided to use pickled peppers instead of raw jalapeños. A whole new egg concept was born.

4 large eggs

3 tablespoons Olive Oil Mayonnaise (page 240)

2 Pickled Peppers (page 232), thinly sliced

Perfect Sauté Seasoning (page 250) or salt and freshly ground white or black pepper

1 Place the eggs in a saucepan; fill with cold water to cover. Bring to a boil over high heat. Remove the pan from the heat, cover, and let stand for 10 minutes. Drain the eggs, then plunge in ice water to cool. Peel and halve lengthwise.

2 Arrange the egg halves yolk side up on a platter. Top each half generously with mayonnaise. Sprinkle the eggs with peppers and seasoning and serve.

VARIATION ▣ EGG SHOOTERS WITH SMOKED TROUT AND TROUT ROE

Substitute crème fraîche for the mayonnaise and omit the peppers and seasoning. Top with 1 ounce flaked smoked trout, 2 tablespoons trout or salmon caviar, and chopped fresh chives.

SPICY CHEESE CRACKERS

With this tasty nibble, it's all about the cheese. If you have a favorite cheddar, go ahead and use it, because the cheese flavor is what makes these crackers destined for greatness. They keep well and are terrific at room temperature, but they are even more amazing hot out of the oven, when the texture is flaky and tender and the cheese flavor is at its most intense. They're just the perfect little bite for a cocktail party; you can make the dough in advance (you can even make it way in advance and freeze it for a month or two) and pop them in the oven at about the time guests are scheduled to arrive. They are so good, you don't even need to top them.

3 cups all-purpose flour

2 teaspoons baking powder

1 teaspoon kosher salt, plus more for sprinkling

½ teaspoon cayenne pepper

1 cup (2 sticks) unsalted butter, cold, cut into cubes

1 pound extra-sharp cheddar cheese, grated (about 4 cups)

¾ pound aged farmhouse cheddar, grated (about 3 cups)

1   In the bowl of an electric mixer fitted with the paddle attachment, blend together the flour, baking powder, salt, and cayenne. Cut in the butter until the mixture is crumbly and resembles coarse meal. Blend in the cheeses; pour in ½ cup cold water until the mixture comes together to form a ball.

2   Transfer the dough to a clean surface. Divide the dough into 2 balls; shape each ball into a 16 × 2-inch log, making each log as uniform as possible. Wrap each log tightly with plastic and refrigerate until firm, at least 1 hour or up to 3 days.

3   Preheat the oven to 400°F.

4   Slice the dough into ¼-inch-thick slabs; transfer to ungreased baking sheets. Sprinkle the tops lightly with salt. Bake until slightly puffed and light golden, about 10 minutes. Transfer the crackers from the baking sheets to wire racks to cool slightly before serving.

TOASTS

As kids, we used to joke that we were going to take toast to the next level. At the time that meant grabbing the rye bread out of the toaster oven at just the right moment, and then, when it was still piping hot, slathering on butter and sprinkling on some salt. You know the aroma of toasted bread? It's just ridiculously good. It was such a simple yet indulgent moment when the timing and the ingredients would come together in just the right way to create this delicious treat, not to mention an unforgettable food memory.

We first got the idea to put variously topped toasts on the menu from a wonderful café in Paris. It was a tiny place that did a great business, always jam-packed with people having a glass of red wine and a piece of bread topped with pâté or ham or cheese, basically small open-faced sandwiches. The great thing about them is that they're not a big commitment. With a regular sandwich you've got double the amount of bread and you are stuck with just that filling, but toasts are smaller and you can snack on a variety of toppings, almost like Spanish tapas or Italian crostini. By our reckoning, these toasts are as American as you can get!

blue ribbon wisdom

CHOOSING YOUR THICKNESS   The thickness of the bread you use for toasts will depend on how you're serving them. If you are making them for a cocktail party as bite-size hors d'oeuvres and you don't want to fill people up, slice the bread thin, about ¼ inch thick. If you're having toasts for lunch, or for something more substantial than a snack, slice the bread ½ to ¾ inch thick.

ROASTED TOMATO, ARUGULA, AND LEMON TOASTS

These toasts are a little lighter than most of the others, and they provide a fresh balance when served with a selection of toasts. The combination of sweet oven-roasted tomatoes, sharp arugula, and bright lemon is excellent.

2½ tablespoons extra-virgin olive oil

2 tablespoons freshly squeezed lemon juice

4 (¼-inch-thick) slices Country White Bread (page 203) or your favorite store-bought crusty loaf of bread, toasted before serving

1 cup Roasted Tomatoes (page 230), roughly chopped

¼ pound fresh arugula (about 4 loosely packed cups)

Perfect Sauté Seasoning (page 251) or salt and freshly ground white or black pepper, for serving

1   In a medium bowl, whisk together the oil and lemon juice.

2   Top each slice of toast generously with tomato, then with arugula. Drizzle the lemon oil over each toast and sprinkle with the seasoning.

STILTON TOASTS
WITH HONEY-PORT GLAZE

The huge wheel of Stilton—the one served with great ceremony at our dad's annual charity fund-raisers and political rallies—was off-limits to us kids. We were told of its great cost, how rare it was outside of England, how Stilton is still made exclusively in the counties of Leicestershire, Nottinghamshire, and Derbyshire, and how only seven dairies are permitted to make the vein-riddled wheel. Images of Rolls-Royces, manicured lawns, and white-gloved butlers were evoked, and when port wine and a special spoon were thrown into the mix, well then, forget it, boys. Dad suggested that the Boursin cheese spread would better suit us if we got peckish. Stilton and port seemed like such an exotic treat when we were growing up that it is a great joy to present it to all in such a simple, everyday manner in this recipe. Toasts make every topping accessible and this is no exception. This mild blue cheese melts gorgeously when topped with a drizzle of warm port glaze.

½ cup nonvintage ruby port

½ cup good-quality honey

4 (¼-inch-thick) slices Country White Bread (page 203) or your favorite store-bought crusty loaf of bread, toasted before serving

½ pound Stilton cheese, crumbled (about 2 cups)

1 TO MAKE THE GLAZE, in a small saucepan over medium heat, combine the port and honey. Bring to a simmer and cook until the sauce is reduced by half, 10 to 12 minutes. Let cool, at least slightly.

2 Top each toast with cheese. Drizzle some of the port glaze over the cheese and serve.

WHOLE ROASTED GARLIC
WITH WARM COUNTRY BREAD TOASTS

SERVES 4

There are few ingredients more alluring and evocative than garlic, and roasted garlic is even one step beyond. Submerged in olive oil and then simmered until the robust cloves become soft and candied and the oil takes on the garlic's aromatic earthiness, our roasted garlic isn't just an elusive flavor hiding in another dish. It *is* the dish, needing nothing more than some toasted country bread and a sprinkle of good salt to shine on its own. Of course, once you start making roasted garlic and get used to having it around, you'll probably start adding it, and its savory oil, to everything you cook. We like to use roasted garlic in any recipe that calls for garlic—in hummus, in Caesar salad, in a pan sauce for lamb. Roasted garlic is much more stable than raw garlic, it has a wonderful sweetness to it, and it doesn't seem to give people the same kind of digestive problems that raw garlic does. Roasted garlic is magic, basically.

8 heads of garlic

Perfect Roast Seasoning (page 250) or kosher salt and freshly ground black pepper

2½ cups extra-virgin olive oil, plus more if needed

1 ounce Parmesan cheese, grated (about ¼ cup)

Lemon wedges, for garnish

4 sprigs of fresh flat-leaf parsley, for garnish

4 (½-inch-thick) slices Country White Bread (page 203) or your favorite store-bought crusty loaf of bread, toasted before serving

1 Preheat the oven to 225°F.

2 Slice off the top third of the garlic heads. Place the garlic in a single layer in a baking dish (the heads should fit closely together) and sprinkle generously with the seasoning. Pour the oil over the garlic and cover the pan with foil. The oil should just cover the garlic. Add more oil if necessary.

3 Bake the garlic until golden and very soft, about 2 hours. Drain off the oil and reserve for another use. Place the garlic heads on a platter. Sprinkle with the Parmesan and garnish the plate with the lemon and parsley. Serve with the warm, toasted bread.

MANCHEGO AND MEXICAN HONEY TOASTS

SERVES 4

One of our culinary rampages through Spain elevated manchego to the forefront of the cheese world for us. It was manchego for breakfast, lunch, and dinner and we never grew weary of its firm, creamy texture and sharp, buttery bite.

Years later, when visiting the honey farm of Felix Vaquero, one of our chefs, in the wildly floral volcanic valley outside of Mexico City, we had another epiphany. Felix's aunt prepared an amazing feast for us, served in a quiet little courtyard flanked by avocado trees, old beehives, and colorful flowers the likes of which we've never seen since. One of the meal's highlights was a local cheese slathered with raw honey. As delicious as this combination was, we couldn't help but think how great the honey would be with our beloved manchego.

4 (¼-inch-thick) slices Country White Bread (page 203) or your favorite store-bought crusty loaf of bread, toasted before serving

2 tablespoons good-quality honey

¼ pound manchego cheese, thinly sliced

Drizzle each slice of toast with the honey, top with manchego cheese, and serve.

MEXICAN HONEY

How did we get into the honey business? Every year after Felix Vaquero would visit his dad in Atlixco, a small town famous for being the flower capital of Mexico, he'd bring us back the most amazing honey we'd ever tasted. Atlixco honeys are crisp, clean, and sweet without being cloying, and each type is unique, from the Golden Reserve Honey, with its light, airy, and buttery texture and an elegant floral bouquet, to the Mt. Mixteca Honey, which is herbaceous and dark with explosive undertones of thyme and lavender. Each variety displays its own one-of-a-kind characteristics that are influenced by so many variables—what kind of flower the honey comes from, the season it was harvested, even the exact location of the valley the flower was growing in. At Blue Ribbon Market we sell five different kinds, and they're available online.

PORK RILLETTES AND CORNICHON TOASTS

Rillettes are another iconic French dish that seems a lot harder to make than it really is. Sort of like a rustic pâté, it's customarily made from pork, duck, or goose—animals with plenty of rich, buttery fat to flavor the mixture. Our version uses both fresh pork and bacon, so it has a smoky undertone that works really nicely with its brawny meatiness. Rillettes have an extensive shelf life. Stored in a sealed jar in the fridge with a little pork fat or duck fat on top, it will keep for weeks, maybe months.

RILLETTES

3 sprigs of fresh thyme

3 sprigs of fresh flat-leaf parsley

2 black peppercorns

1 bay leaf

2 pounds pork shoulder butt, cut into 2-inch pieces

⅓ pound slab bacon, cut into 2-inch cubes

1 head of garlic, cut in half crosswise

2 tablespoons kosher salt

TOASTS

10 (1-inch-thick) slices Country White Bread (page 203) or your favorite store-bought crusty loaf of bread, toasted before serving

2 tablespoons whole-grain mustard

⅓ cup finely chopped cornichons

Fleur de sel or other good-quality coarse sea salt, for serving

Extra-virgin olive oil, for serving

Chopped fresh flat-leaf parsley leaves, for garnish

1 Preheat the oven to 375°F. Cut out a piece of parchment to fit inside a Dutch oven or deep baking dish.

2 MAKE A SACHET: In a small square of cheesecloth (or alternatively, in a tea ball), tie together the thyme, parsley, peppercorns, and bay leaf. Put the sachet in the Dutch oven.

3 Add the pork butt pieces, bacon, garlic, and salt; toss to combine. Pour in 1 cup water.

4 Cover with the prepared piece of parchment. Braise in the oven until the pork is very tender and falling apart, 2 to 3 hours. Remove the sachet and garlic; let the pork cool to room temperature.

5   In the bowl of an electric mixer fitted with the paddle attachment, whip the meat until the mixture is creamy but still has some small chunks. (Alternatively, if you like chunkier rillettes, you can mash the pork roughly with a potato masher or fork.) You can make this up to a month ahead. Store it in the refrigerator, protected with a layer of pork fat or duck fat if possible, in a tightly covered container.

6   To serve, spread toasted bread slices with a thin layer of mustard. Spread about 3 tablespoons of rillettes over the mustard. Sprinkle with cornichons and fleur de sel. Drizzle lightly with oil and garnish with parsley. Cut the toasts into quarters, or, if serving as hors d'oeuvres, into eighths.

GOAT CHEESE TOASTS
WITH GRILLED RED ONION AND ROASTED TOMATO

SERVES 4

Tangy, aged goat cheese stands up to the robust flavors of onion and tomatoes in this tasty snack.

1 red onion, peeled and thickly sliced

1 tablespoon olive oil

2 ounces watercress (about 2 cups loosely packed)

4 (¼-inch-thick) slices Country White Bread (page 203) or your favorite store-bought crusty loaf of bread, toasted before serving

½ cup Roasted Tomatoes (page 230), chopped

6 ounces Crottin de Chavignol, Bûcheron, or other good-quality, firm goat cheese, thinly sliced

Pinch of fleur de sel or other good-quality coarse sea salt, for serving

Freshly ground black pepper, for serving

Extra-virgin olive oil, for serving

1 Preheat a grill, grill pan, or broiler. Brush the onion slices with the oil and grill or broil, turning once, until golden brown and tender, about 7 minutes. Let cool, then roughly chop.

2 In a small bowl, toss together 3 tablespoons of the chopped onion with the watercress (reserve the remaining onion for another use). Spread each bread slice with tomatoes. Top with cheese and the watercress mixture. Season with salt and pepper. Drizzle with extra-virgin olive oil and serve.

DUCK CONFIT AND DIJON MUSTARD TOASTS

SERVES 4 TO 6

D uck confit is a traditional French delicacy, one that is hard to forget after cooking and eating in France for any length of time. For us, it epitomizes the very best of French culinary tradition; it was one of the dishes that drove us to become chefs. It was so good we just had to learn how to cook it ourselves. Confit may be a project that takes a couple of days, but it's a fun process and isn't at all tricky or difficult. Plus most of the time is spent simply allowing the ingredients to do their thing, like salting the duck legs and letting them sit. Salting the duck both seasons the meat and pulls the liquid out of it, which results in a very rich flavor and texture after the duck cooks slowly for hours. That's why duck confit is more special than just cooked duck legs. Confiting is a technique we love because it shows that cooking isn't simply about subjecting an ingredient to heat and then serving it right away. Some dishes need a little more time and effort, and they're all the more grand for that.

This is a terrific and simple way to serve duck confit: just spread it on bread with mustard. But confit is also great served with salad: gently heat the meat in a skillet first to warm it, then toss it with greens and our House Vinaigrette (page 244).

4 moulard duck legs (about 2 pounds), rinsed and patted dry but not trimmed

Perfect Roast Seasoning (page 250) or kosher salt and freshly ground black pepper

4 (¼-inch-thick) slices Country White Bread (page 203) or your favorite store-bought crusty loaf of bread, toasted before serving

4 teaspoons Dijon mustard

Chopped fresh flat-leaf parsley leaves, for garnish

4 teaspoons extra-virgin olive oil, for serving

1 TO MAKE THE CONFIT: Sprinkle the duck generously with the seasoning. Place the duck legs in a pan in one layer. Cover tightly with plastic wrap and refrigerate for 24 hours.

2 The next day, preheat the oven to 325°F.

3   Place the duck legs, fat side down, in a 9-inch ovenproof skillet or similar-size pan (the legs should fit snugly in a single layer). Heat the duck legs over medium-high heat until the fat starts to render. When there is about ¼ inch of rendered fat in the pan, cover it with foil and place it in the oven. Let roast for 2 hours. Remove the foil and continue roasting until the duck is golden brown, about 1 hour more.

4   Let the duck cool in the fat, then strain off the fat, and reserve. Remove the skin from the duck and use for another purpose (see Blue Ribbon Wisdom). Pull the duck meat off the bones, shredding it into bite-size pieces as you work. Set aside 1½ cups (about 6 ounces) of the meat for the toasts. Transfer any remaining duck to an airtight container and pour strained fat over the duck to cover. (Reserve any remaining strained fat for another use; see Blue Ribbon Wisdom.)

5   TO ASSEMBLE THE TOASTS: Spread each toast slice evenly with mustard. Top with duck confit. Sprinkle each toast with parsley, drizzle with oil, and serve.

6   You can make duck confit up to a month ahead. Store it in the refrigerator, then reheat in a 400°F oven until crisped, about 15 minutes.

blue ribbon wisdom

DUCK FAT Another joy of duck confit is that you're left with all this glorious duck fat and skin. We love to sauté with the fat because it can take a good amount of heat without smoking and it gives everything such a rich and crispy texture without being greasy or heavy. Crunchy Potato Cakes (page 123), sautéed in duck fat instead of butter, are just a sublime experience, and you can also use the fat to sauté shrimp or firm fish. We love to use it mixed with extra-virgin olive oil in salad dressing. It imparts a subtle smoky flavor, perfect for a warm vinaigrette drizzled over hearty greens such as frisée, spinach, or radicchio. And the skin is great tossed with salad or sprinkled over mashed potatoes, eggs, or anywhere you'd put bacon.

COUNTRY PÂTÉ AND SHALLOT CONFIT TOASTS

SERVES 12 TO 16

We find that most pâté recipes are overly fussy. After all, what is pâté? It is basically meat loaf—the best meat loaf in the world, granted—and as such the recipe for it should be just as simple as for meat loaf; if it were, we bet more people would make their own pâtés. So that's what we set out to do here. The technique is straightforward as can be: you grind up a combination of meats and flavorings in the food processor, then bake them in a water bath. We add both pork butt and bacon to keep the mixture moist and smooth, and some shallot confit for a sweet, onion flavor. You can skip the shallot confit to make things even easier. Just sauté chopped shallot in oil until soft and sweet, and use that instead.

PÂTÉ

1 pound pork shoulder butt, cold, cut into 1-inch chunks

1 pound veal shoulder, cold, cut into 1-inch chunks

1 pound chicken livers, cold, connecting veins between lobes removed

1 pound bacon, cold, cut into 1-inch chunks

2 large eggs, lightly beaten

2 tablespoons chopped fresh thyme leaves

½ tablespoon chopped Shallot Confit (page 235)

1 tablespoon salt

½ teaspoon freshly ground black pepper

½ teaspoon five-spice powder

TOASTS

1 loaf Country White Bread (page 203) or your favorite store-bought crusty loaf of bread, toasted before serving

Dijon mustard, for serving

Chopped fresh flat-leaf parsley leaves, for garnish

Fleur de sel or other good-quality coarse sea salt, for serving

Extra-virgin olive oil, for serving

1 Place a medium mixing bowl in the refrigerator to chill. Preheat the oven to 350°F.

2 Combine the pork, veal, chicken livers, and bacon in the chilled bowl. In a food processor fitted with the blade attachment, pulse the meat in small batches until well ground. Turn the mixture out into a large bowl. Add the eggs, thyme, shallot confit, salt, pepper, and five-spice powder, stirring well to combine.

3   Press the mixture into a 9 × 5-inch loaf pan. Place the pan inside a large roasting pan and fill the roasting pan with hot water to come halfway up the sides of the loaf pan. Cover loosely with foil and bake until a thermometer inserted into the pâté registers 160°F, 1½ to 2 hours. Remove from the water bath. Let cool at room temperature. Cover with plastic wrap and refrigerate overnight or at least 6 hours before serving.

4   To serve, unmold by inverting the pan onto a plate and gently dumping out the pâté, and slice the pâté ¼ inch thick (or slice it in the pan). Spread the slices of toasted bread evenly with mustard. Top with slices of pâté. Sprinkle the pâté with parsley and fleur de sel, drizzle with oil, and cut the toasts into quarters on the diagonal.

blue ribbon wisdom

PORK BUTT Understanding the ins and outs of cuts of pork can be confusing, especially since many cuts are very similar or go by a variety of names. When it comes to slow cooking, it is most important to remember this: always go for a cut from the shoulder butt (also sometimes referred to as simply pork butt or pork shoulder). This is the top portion of the front leg of the hog, and because it is marbled with fat, it becomes meltingly tender when cooked slowly over low heat. If we had to pick one particular shoulder cut to braise for the rest of time, we'd choose the Boston pork butt, which is cut from the upper portion of the pig's shoulder.

The other great thing about pork butt is that it is not fancy or expensive, which means you can find it in just about any supermarket. You can roast it slowly at low heat, or if you're short on time, fast at a high heat. Basically, you just can't mess up pork butt.

ARUGULA, RED PEPPER, AND GOAT CHEESE FLATBREAD

MAKES 2 (10 X 15-INCH) FLATBREADS

When Bruce was learning the bread baking trade at Poilâne in Paris, he was taught to test the temperature of the oven by cutting off small pieces of dough and throwing them in to bake on the oven floor before loading in the rest of the bread. It was a great trick to make sure the oven was hot enough in the days before oven thermometers, and it also gave the baker a little snack when those pieces of dough came out. Crisp on the outside, chewy on the inside, these flatbreads would get slathered with whatever tasty ingredient was on hand, from butter to cheese to Nutella.

Our flatbreads keep that same tradition of using regular bread dough as a base, and then mixing in whatever we have on hand. We've experimented with everything from seafood to sliced meats and vegetables, but often keep things as simple as just a little coarse sea salt and rosemary. Any way you flavor them, they're a baker's delight.

Dough for Country White Bread (page 203), through second rise

4 ounces fresh goat cheese (about 2 cups)

1 cup sliced arugula

⅓ cup Roasted Red Peppers (page 231), cut into ¼-inch strips

Flour, for dusting

Extra-virgin olive oil, for brushing

Kosher salt, for sprinkling

1 Put the dough in the bowl of an electric mixer with a hook attachment. Add the goat cheese, arugula, and red peppers. Mix on medium speed until the ingredients are combined, about 10 minutes. You may need to stop the mixer several times to scrape down the sides.

2 Preheat the oven to 500°F.

3 Turn the dough out onto a lightly floured surface and divide into 2 equal pieces. Roll each piece into a ¼-inch-thick rectangle. Transfer the dough to baking sheets and brush with oil and sprinkle with salt. Bake until golden brown and slightly crisp, 15 to 20 minutes. Transfer to a wire rack to cool and serve warm or at room temperature.

BACON AND RED ONION FLATBREAD

Here's another of our favorite flatbread variations. This one stays nice and moist from the red onions—and the bacon.

¼ pound slab bacon, cut into ½-inch cubes (about 1 cup)

1 small red onion, peeled and cut into chunks

1 tablespoon extra-virgin olive oil, plus additional for brushing

Dough for Country White Bread (page 203), through second rise

Flour, for dusting

Kosher salt, for sprinkling

1 Preheat the oven to 350°F.

2 Combine the bacon and onion on a rimmed baking sheet and drizzle with the oil. Bake for 15 to 20 minutes, until the bacon cubes are brown and crisp and the onion chunks are tender. Carefully transfer the bacon and onion with the fat to a bowl and allow to cool to room temperature.

3 Put the dough in the bowl of an electric mixer with a hook attachment. Add the bacon, onion, and accumulated fat and juices and mix until combined, about 10 minutes.

4 Preheat the oven to 500°F.

5 Turn the dough out onto a lightly floured surface and divide into 2 equal pieces. Roll each piece into a ¼-inch-thick rectangle. Transfer the dough to baking sheets and brush with additional olive oil and sprinkle with salt. Bake until golden brown and crisp, 10 to 15 minutes. Transfer to a wire rack to cool and serve warm or at room temperature.

VARIATION ▣ OLIVE FLATBREAD

Omit the bacon and onion and mix 1 cup sliced kalamata olives into the dough.

MATZOH

We've been fascinated with matzoh since we took our first trip to Israel for Eric's bar mitzvah and saw people cooking their own matzoh in little cast-iron ovens set over a fire. We thought it was so cool that anyone would cook bread right out on the street. Back home in Jersey, matzoh was a once-a-year treat, something we had only around Passover. We'd grab the boxes of regular and egg-and-onion matzoh as soon as they hit the shelves, and try to hoard them as long as we could. When we opened Blue Ribbon Bakery, with its great brick oven, we knew we wanted to start making our own matzoh and have it more than just once a year. It's such a great, cracker-like snack and a very simple recipe, basically just flour, water, and salt. Make this once and you may never go back to the boxed kind again.

1 cup all-purpose flour, plus more for dusting

½ teaspoon kosher salt, plus additional for sprinkling

Extra-virgin olive oil, for brushing

1   Preheat the oven to 500°F.

2   In the bowl of an electric mixer with a hook attachment, combine the flour and salt with ½ cup water. Mix on medium speed until the dough comes together in a ball, about 10 minutes.

3   Turn the dough out onto a lightly floured surface and divide into 12 equal pieces. Roll each piece into a rectangle about ⅛ inch thick, then prick the dough all over with a fork. Brush each piece lightly with oil and sprinkle with salt.

4   Bake the crackers in batches, if necessary, on the floor of the oven until golden brown and very crisp, 8 to 10 minutes. Transfer the matzoh to a wire rack to cool completely. Store in an airtight container at room temperature for up to 10 days.

appetizers, soups, and salads

◙ clams with roasted tomatoes, cilantro, and toasted baguette
◙ garlic shrimp with chorizo ◙ crispy fried salt-and-pepper
shrimp with spicy wilted lettuce ◙ sautéed calamari with
parsley and garlic ◙ grilled chicken wings with homemade hot
sauce and blue cheese ◙ pupu platter: spicy glazed ribs, pierogi,
egg rolls, and chicken skewers ◙ comforting cream of tomato
soup ◙ smoky bacon and garlic soup ◙ martha's excellent
matzoh ball soup ◙ blue ribbon hummus ◙ grilled and
marinated crudités ◙ roasted garlic caesar salad ◙ baby
arugula and butternut squash salad with manchego and balsamic
vinaigrette ◙ market salad ◙ smoked trout salad with granny
smith apple, endive, watercress, and creamy dill dressing

Appetizers are the fun part of a meal; whether they're informally passed around the table or artfully arranged on individual platters, they're what make a dinner special. Think about it this way: since nobody is eating them for sustenance alone, they come to the table for pure enjoyment.

When people go out to a restaurant, whether it's Blue Ribbon or someplace else, they almost always order an appetizer or two to start out the experience. But it's rare that home cooks treat themselves and their guests to a little bite to whet the appetite for the main course to come. We understand: it can seem overwhelming to attempt to create another course on top of the main course (including one or two side dishes) and a dessert. But when an appetizer—be it a soup, a salad, or just a tasty little nosh—is presented the whole meal immediately perks up, becomes an event. A night around the family dinner table begins to feel like a special occasion.

When you're cooking at home, don't let yourself fall into the no-starter trap. On the contrary, you could even make a full meal out of just the app menu, especially when you're serving something like our Pupu Platter with Spicy Glazed Ribs, Pierogi, Egg Rolls, and Chicken Skewers (page 56). Depending on how many people you're making it for, it can really be an entire meal on a plate. Recipes such as Clams with Roasted Tomatoes, Cilantro, and Toasted Baguette (page 46) and Grilled Chicken Wings with Homemade Hot Sauce and Blue Cheese (page 54) are perfect for cocktail parties, while Smoky Bacon and Garlic Soup (page 63) and Roasted Garlic Caesar Salad (page 72) will work really well for a quiet evening at home.

CLAMS
WITH ROASTED TOMATOES, CILANTRO, AND TOASTED BAGUETTE

A boldly flavored appetizer, this has its deepest roots in Amagansett on Long Island, where we spent a chunk of our summer vacations. Our dad loved to undertake elaborate cooking projects that often included the local clams, which he showed us how to clean and shuck. Then we'd marvel at his giant bubbling pots of cioppino or *zuppa di pesce*. The flavors of this dish, though, are inspired from our trips through Europe and they work really well together; the brininess of the clams mixes with the sweetness of the roasted tomatoes and the earthiness of the cilantro to create a balance of sweet and savory. You could say this dish is like the Costa Brava meets Provence meets Amagansett. It will work well with any kind of clam, or even with tiny cockles.

12 Manila or littleneck clams (1½ to 2 pounds), scrubbed well

4 tablespoons extra-virgin olive oil

¼ cup thinly sliced garlic (from about 5 fat cloves)

¼ cup Roasted Tomatoes (page 230), chopped

2 tablespoons chopped fresh flat-leaf parsley leaves

2 tablespoons chopped fresh cilantro leaves

¼ teaspoon Perfect Sauté Seasoning (page 251) or salt and freshly ground white or black pepper

1 small baguette, halved lengthwise

Garlic oil (page 235) or extra-virgin olive oil, for brushing

1   Fill a large stockpot with ½ inch water. Bring to a simmer over medium-high heat. Add the clams and cook, covered, for about 10 minutes, until all the clams have opened. Check occasionally during the cooking time and remove clams as they open (see Blue Ribbon Wisdom). Use a slotted spoon to transfer the clams to a large bowl. Discard any that do not open after 10 to 12 minutes.

2   In a large skillet, heat 2 tablespoons of the olive oil over medium-high heat. Add the garlic and cook until the garlic is just beginning to color, 1 to 2 minutes. Remove the pan from the heat and stir in the remaining 2 tablespoons

recipe continues

olive oil, the tomatoes, parsley, cilantro, and seasoning. Pour the mixture evenly over the clams and toss gently; taste and correct the seasoning if need be. Let stand at room temperature while you prepare the baguette.

3   Heat a grill pan until very hot. Brush the cut side of the baguette with garlic oil. Grill the baguette until lightly charred, about 2 minutes per side. Serve the clams with the bread alongside for soaking up juices.

blue ribbon wisdom

PURGING SHELLFISH Whenever you buy clams, mussels, scallops, or anything else sold in the shell, you'll need to purge them of all the sand they've ingested. To do this, put the shellfish in a bowl of heavily salted water (use table salt so it will dissolve quickly) and let them sit, changing the water every 15 minutes. You'll know they're clean when there's no more sand at the bottom of the bowl, which could take anywhere from 30 minutes to 2 hours, depending on how sandy they were to begin with. It's important to make sure the water you use is as salty as seawater so the shellfish stay alive. Don't put them in fresh water or they'll die.

DON'T OVERCOOK CLAMS The way to avoid rubbery clams is not to overcook them. As soon as they open, they're ready. If your stove doesn't have a very strong flame and you have a lot of clams, they can cook unevenly, with the clams at the bottom of the pot opening a lot faster than the ones on top. If you find yourself in that situation, make sure to stir the clams every minute or so. As they open, transfer them to a separate pot or a bowl with a cover. That way you won't overcook the first clams that open while waiting for the rest to catch up.

GARLIC SHRIMP
WITH CHORIZO

In August 1994, we closed the doors of Blue Ribbon for two weeks and headed off to Spain with the crew. Everyone piled into a Euro van, and off we went in search of great food and wine. One lucky night in Haro, Rioja, we stumbled into a tiny tapas bar called Chamonix. At first glance it was a pretty unimpressive place, cramped and hot and smoky. But the tapas sent out by the friendly folks at the bar were transcendent, and those flavors still influence our cooking today, especially the combination of garlic, shrimp, and chorizo. The quality of the chorizo is of the utmost importance in this dish; if you use a good, spicy piece of chorizo and some nice sweet shrimp, you can't go wrong.

5 ounces jumbo shrimp (about 6 pieces), peeled and deveined

4 ounces Spanish chorizo (about 2 small links), quartered lengthwise and cut into ½-inch chunks

2 medium garlic cloves, thinly sliced

1 tablespoon garlic oil (page 235) or extra-virgin olive oil

Pinch of Perfect Sauté Seasoning (page 251) or salt and freshly ground white or black pepper

Chopped fresh flat-leaf parsley leaves, for garnish

1 Preheat the oven to 425°F.

2 In a bowl, toss together the shrimp, chorizo, garlic, oil, and seasoning. Transfer to a small, ovenproof dish or earthenware crock. Bake until the shrimp are just cooked through, 7 to 10 minutes. Sprinkle with the parsley and serve.

NOTE In the States, you can generally find chorizo two ways: dried (and cured) or fresh. We call for Spanish chorizo, which is sold dried and cured with garlic, salt, and smoked paprika to give it its characteristic red color. It's the easiest to find and is usually available in large supermarkets and Spanish specialty shops. Fresh chorizo, which you might also see, is similarly spiced. The big difference is that the pork is raw and has not been cured, and therefore needs to be fully cooked before eating. It has a crumbly texture just like an Italian or breakfast sausage. While both chorizos are great, don't substitute one for the other.

CRISPY FRIED SALT-AND-PEPPER SHRIMP
WITH SPICY WILTED LETTUCE

SERVES 2 TO 4

When we were kids, on Saturday mornings we'd make the trip with our dad from New Jersey to the bustling streets of Chinatown in Manhattan. Going from quiet, tree-lined suburbia to the vibrant chaos of Mon Bo Rice Shop was like taking a day trip to another planet. Cooks yelled, glasses crashed, waiters zipped around carrying sizzling food high over their heads. We'd devour plump and crispy salt-and-pepper shrimp, shells and all. In our version, we use fresh Louisiana shrimp and serve them on wilted iceberg lettuce studded with serrano chiles.

2½ tablespoons coarse salt

1 tablespoon crushed red pepper flakes

1½ teaspoons black sesame seeds

5 ounces jumbo shrimp (about 6 pieces)

1 teaspoon canola oil, plus more for deep-frying

2 cups sliced iceberg lettuce

1 teaspoon chopped serrano chile

½ teaspoon Perfect Sauté Seasoning (page 251) or salt and freshly ground white or black pepper

Ponzu Sauce (recipe follows)

1   Combine the salt, red pepper flakes, and sesame seeds in a small bowl.

2   Using kitchen shears, cut through the shell on the back of each shrimp, and remove the thick black vein with the tip of a knife. Do not remove the shell.

3   Fill a medium pot halfway (about 3 inches) with canola oil and heat until a deep-fat thermometer reads 375°F. Fry the shrimp until golden and just cooked through, about 2 minutes. Transfer to a paper-towel-lined plate to drain and sprinkle immediately with some of the spicy salt mixture.

4   While the shrimp fry, heat the teaspoon of oil in a medium skillet over medium-high heat. Add the lettuce, serrano chile, and seasoning. Cook, stirring, until the lettuce is wilted, about 45 seconds.

5   Arrange the lettuce on a platter. Top with the shrimp. Serve with a ramekin of ponzu sauce on the side, and pass the remaining spicy salt and pepper mixture.

PONZU SAUCE

MAKES ABOUT 2½ CUPS

¾ cup soy sauce

¾ cup rice wine vinegar

6 tablespoons mirin

3 tablespoons sake

1 (1-inch) strip of kombu

1 tablespoon bonito flakes

¼ orange, peeled and cut into segments

Combine the soy sauce, vinegar, mirin, sake, kombu, bonito flakes, and orange in a jar and stir well. Cover and refrigerate for at least 2 days and up to a week.

SAUTÉED CALAMARI
WITH PARSLEY AND GARLIC

|||||||||||||||||
SERVES 4
|||||||||||||||||

At staff mealtime on particularly busy days at Le Recamier restaurant in Paris, Chef Robert would call for calamari, plenty of minced garlic, a handful of roughly chopped parsley, and a very hot pan. A few minutes later, everyone in the kitchen would dig into this amazingly flavorful dish. Before that time, we had never in our life tasted squid that hadn't been deep-fried, and we were just stunned by how good it was, especially when combined with garlic and parsley. That dish really made an impression on us, and it's been a favorite of the Blue Ribbon faithful now for more than fifteen years. For the best result, buy the smallest calamari available and have all your ingredients at the ready before you start heating the pan. Once you add the calamari to the pan, don't take your eyes off it. As soon as it's opaque, it's done.

1 tablespoon extra-virgin olive oil

1 pound baby squid, cleaned (if using larger squid, cut bodies into ¾-inch rings; leave tentacles whole)

2 tablespoons unsalted butter

2 teaspoons chopped garlic

1 tablespoon chopped fresh flat-leaf parsley leaves

½ teaspoon Perfect Sauté Seasoning (page 251), or more to taste, or salt and freshly ground white or black pepper

Add the oil to the skillet, and heat over high heat until it begins to smoke. Carefully add the squid, butter, garlic, parsley, and seasoning. Cook, tossing frequently, until the squid is opaque and cooked through, 3 to 4 minutes. Taste and sprinkle with additional seasoning if needed.

GRILLED CHICKEN WINGS
WITH HOMEMADE HOT SAUCE AND BLUE CHEESE

SERVES 2 TO 4

At Blue Ribbon, one of our main culinary goals is to take all the dishes that we loved from childhood and elevate them. Chicken wings are no exception. Broiled or grilled instead of deep-fried, and seasoned with homemade hot sauce spiked with plum sauce and brown sugar, these crispy, tangy, spicy wings are like the best Buffalo chicken wings you've ever tasted, maybe even better.

8 chicken wings (about 1¾ pounds)

Perfect Roast Seasoning (page 250) or kosher salt and freshly ground black pepper

2 tablespoons Blue Ribbon Hot Sauce (page 242) or your favorite bottled hot sauce

2 tablespoons unsalted butter, melted

1 tablespoon Chinese plum sauce

1½ teaspoons light brown sugar

¼ cup sour cream

¼ cup crumbled blue cheese

1   Sprinkle the chicken wings with the seasoning. Let rest for 20 minutes.

2   In the meantime, preheat the broiler or grill.

3   In a small bowl, mix together the hot sauce, butter, plum sauce, and brown sugar. Set aside half of the hot sauce.

4   Broil or grill the wings, turning once, for 20 minutes. Slather the wings with the remaining half of the hot sauce mixture, making sure to coat both sides of the wings. Broil or grill until glazed and crispy, 10 to 15 minutes longer, turning once. Using a clean utensil, brush the wings with the reserved hot sauce mixture before serving.

5   TO MAKE THE DRESSING: Mix together the sour cream and blue cheese. Serve with the wings.

PUPU PLATTER
SPICY GLAZED RIBS, PIEROGI, EGG ROLLS, AND CHICKEN SKEWERS

PLATTER SERVES 16; INDIVIDUAL RECIPES SERVE 4 TO 6

In Manhattan's Chinatown, Mott Street was definitely our number one choice for Asian fare when we were growing up. But not far behind, and only fifteen minutes from home in New Jersey, was Oriental Yum Yum. I can't say that everything that came out of that kitchen was "yum yum," but few dishes ever had more of an impact on us Brombergs than the pupu platters that strip mall restaurant could turn out. Could there be anything better? Fried, baked, roasted. Pork, shrimp, beef, egg rolls, spareribs. And best of all: fire! You actually got to play with fire in front of your parents and it was okay . . . up to a point, anyway. The combinations of sauce and meat and levels of char seemed endless and mind-boggling.

Our Blue Ribbon version keeps the interactive spirit of the dish, but expands the food offerings: chicken egg rolls, chicken skewers, spareribs, and potato pierogi (an homage to our beloved Polish housekeeper Gladys Czak).

This is what cooking is all about to us . . . fun, fun, fun!

SPICY GLAZED RIBS

SERVES 4 TO 6

3 pounds (1 slab) St. Louis–cut pork spareribs

Perfect Roast Seasoning (page 250) or kosher salt and freshly ground black pepper

2 tablespoons cider vinegar

1½ cups barbecue sauce, homemade (page 243) or purchased, plus more for serving

1   Preheat the oven to 300°F.

2   Season the meat generously all over with the seasoning. Place in a large roasting pan. Add 2 tablespoons water and the vinegar to the bottom of the pan; cover the pan tightly with foil. Bake, turning every hour, until the ribs are fork

tender, about 3 hours. Remove from the pan and cool completely. The ribs can be made up to 24 hours before serving and refrigerated until ready to grill.

3   Preheat a grill or the broiler. Slice the meat into individual ribs. Toss gently with the barbecue sauce. If broiling, line a large rimmed baking sheet with foil and arrange the ribs in a single layer on the baking sheet. Grill or broil, turning once, until glazed and slightly charred, 4 to 5 minutes per side. Serve, with additional sauce on the side.

PIEROGI

MAKES ABOUT 2 DOZEN PIEROGI; SERVES 4 TO 6

DOUGH

4 cups all-purpose flour, plus more for dusting

1½ teaspoons salt

1¼ cups (2½ sticks) unsalted butter, chilled and cubed

⅔ cup sour cream

1 large egg, lightly beaten

ONION CONFIT

6 medium onions, halved and thinly sliced

8 tablespoons (1 stick) unsalted butter

FILLING

1 pound medium white potatoes, peeled

½ teaspoon Perfect Sauté Seasoning (page 251) or salt and freshly ground white or black pepper

1 large egg, whisked with 1 tablespoon water

Canola oil, for deep-frying (optional)

Sour cream, for serving

Onion confit, for serving

1   TO MAKE THE DOUGH: In the bowl of an electric mixer fitted with the paddle attachment, briefly mix together the flour and salt. Add the butter cubes and blend until the mixture resembles coarse meal, about 2 minutes. Mix in the sour cream and the egg. Continue to beat until the dough comes together. Form the dough into 2 equal balls. Flatten each ball into a disk using your palm, wrap in plastic, and refrigerate for at least 2 hours and up to 2 days.

2   TO MAKE THE ONION CONFIT: Combine the onions and butter in a very large skillet or Dutch oven over medium heat. Cook, stirring frequently, until the onions

recipe continues

become dark and sweet, 1½ to 2 hours. The onion confit can be made up to 1 week ahead and refrigerated in an airtight container. Let come to room temperature before using.

3   TO MAKE THE FILLING: Put the potatoes in a pot of salted water and bring to a boil. Cook until tender, 30 to 45 minutes. Drain and let cool. Grate the potatoes into a bowl. Stir in 1½ cups of the onion confit (reserve additional confit for serving) and the seasoning.

4   To assemble the pierogi, line a rimmed baking sheet with parchment or wax paper. On a lightly floured surface, roll 1 dough ball out until ⅛ inch thick. Use a 4-inch round cookie cutter to stamp out circles of dough (or use a knife to cut out 4-inch rounds).

5   Fill half of each dough circle with 2 teaspoons of the filling, leaving a ⅛-inch border of dough around the edges. Brush the border with the egg wash. Fold the other half of dough over the filling and press well to seal. Crimp the edges with a fork. Transfer the pierogi to the prepared baking sheet. Repeat with the remaining dough ball and filling. Freeze the pierogi for 30 minutes or up to 1 month, well covered.

6   Bring a large pot of water to a boil. Have a large bowl of ice water ready. Working in two batches, drop frozen pierogi into the boiling water. When the water returns to a boil (this should take 1 to 2 minutes), remove the pierogi with a slotted spoon and drop into the ice water to stop the cooking. Drain the pierogi and transfer to a baking sheet lined with lightly greased wax paper until ready to use (up to 2 hours). Keep the pierogi covered with a slightly damp kitchen towel or with another sheet of lightly greased wax paper.

7   If frying the pierogi, fill a large pot with oil about 3 inches deep and heat until a deep-fat thermometer reads 375°F. Fry the pierogi, in batches, until golden and cooked through, 3 to 4 minutes. Drain on a paper-towel-lined plate.

If steaming the pierogi, in a large pot, bring 1 inch water to a simmer over medium-high heat. Working in batches, place one layer of the pierogi in a steamer basket and cook, covered, until the pierogi are cooked through, about 10 minutes.

8   Serve hot, with sour cream and the remaining onion confit on the side.

recipe continues

EGG ROLLS

1 tablespoon unsalted butter

½ tablespoon sesame oil

2 tablespoons finely chopped garlic

2 tablespoons finely chopped peeled fresh ginger

1 pound ground dark-meat chicken

3 ounces cremini mushrooms, finely chopped (about 1 cup)

2 tablespoons chopped celery leaves

½ tablespoon hoisin sauce

¼ teaspoon Perfect Sauté Seasoning (page 251) or salt and freshly ground white or black pepper

1 dozen wonton wrappers

1 large egg, whisked with 1 tablespoon water

Canola oil, for deep-frying

Hot Chinese mustard or plum sauce, for serving

1 TO MAKE THE FILLING: Heat the butter and sesame oil in a large skillet over medium-high heat. Add the garlic and ginger and cook, stirring, for 2 minutes. Add the chicken and mushrooms and cook until the chicken is cooked through and most of the liquid in the pan has evaporated, 8 to 10 minutes. Remove from the heat and stir in the celery leaves, hoisin sauce, and seasoning. Let the mixture cool to room temperature (the filling can be made up to 3 days ahead and refrigerated in an airtight container until ready to use).

2 Lay out 1 wonton wrapper in front of you so that it looks like a diamond (instead of a square). Spoon about 2 tablespoons filling along the end closest to you and fold the bottom of the wrapper up over the mixture. Fold the left and right corners toward the center and continue to roll away from you. Brush a bit of the egg wash on the edges of the roll to help seal. Repeat with the remaining wonton wrappers and filling. After being filled, the wontons can be covered and refrigerated for up to 3 days or frozen for up to 2 weeks.

3 Meanwhile, fill a large pot with canola oil about 3 inches deep and heat until a deep-fat thermometer reads 375°F.

4 Fry the egg rolls, in batches if necessary, until golden all over, 3 to 4 minutes. Drain on a paper-towel-lined plate. Serve hot with hot Chinese mustard.

CHICKEN SKEWERS

Canola oil, for deep-frying

¼ cup all-purpose flour

1 pound ground chicken

½ cup barbecue sauce, homemade (page 243) or purchased

1 Fill a large, deep pot with oil about 4 inches deep and heat until a deep-fat thermometer reads 375°F. Preheat the broiler. Place the flour in a wide shallow bowl.

2 Dust your hands lightly with flour and form about 2 tablespoons chicken in a torpedo shape around the end of each of 16 metal skewers. Dip the chicken in flour to coat, tapping off any excess.

3 Submerge the chicken-coated ends of the skewers in the hot oil and fry until the chicken is golden and cooked through, 2 to 3 minutes. Drain on a paper-towel-lined tray.

4 Baste the chicken with the barbecue sauce. Broil on a foil-lined rimmed baking sheet until glazed, 1 to 2 minutes, watching carefully to see that they do not burn. Serve hot.

COMFORTING CREAM OF TOMATO SOUP

SERVES 4

This recipe goes straight back to our youngest days, when we'd dip grilled cheese sandwiches into hot bowls of the cream of tomato soup our mom used to make in the cold New Jersey winters. Mom's recipe was straight out of the can; but even so, that steaming, savory soup epitomized warmth, which we always looked forward to as we peeled off frozen scarves, hats, and gloves. I suppose that's why a generation later it's still eagerly anticipated by our own kids—and by the inner kids of all our customers as well.

As far as cream soups go, this is lighter than most, thanks to the acidity of the tomatoes, which balances the richness of the cream. If you want an even lighter soup, substitute vegetable broth or water for some of the heavy cream. Don't even think about using milk. It's less stable than heavy cream and might curdle when heated. We get a lot of requests, including from Bruce's wife, Kerry, for a cream-free version. Using more broth or water instead of cream makes a pretty intense soup that is just as good in its own way.

2 tablespoons unsalted butter	1 (32-ounce) can crushed tomatoes
1 Spanish onion, thinly sliced	¾ to 1¼ cups heavy cream, to taste
Kosher salt	

1   In a large nonreactive stockpot over medium heat, melt the butter. Add the onion and a pinch of salt and toss well. Reduce the heat to medium-low, cover, and cook, stirring occasionally, until the onion is meltingly tender, lowering the heat, about 15 minutes.

2   Add the tomatoes and 4 cups water and raise the heat to bring the mixture to a simmer. Simmer, uncovered, for 20 minutes. Transfer to a blender and carefully puree until smooth, working in batches if necessary. The soup can be refrigerated, covered, for up to 3 days. Return the soup to the pan.

3   Stir in the cream and season with salt to taste. Gently heat the soup until steaming and serve.

SMOKY BACON AND GARLIC SOUP

Some recipes are born out of circumstance, necessity, and more than a little garlic. This is one of those recipes, created when our partner Sefton Stallard wanted to find a dish that would use up all the potato scraps we'd accumulate throughout the day. Usually, those misshapen, unwanted—you could even say unloved—scraps ended up in staff meals. But one day, without warning, Sefton decided to put them to better use. He threw some bacon, onions, and garlic into sizzling olive oil in a giant cauldron. He added wine and mountains of potato scraps, then let everything simmer until all the flavors came together into a fragrant, harmonious whole. This garlicky soup has since become a headliner at our wine bar—not bad for potato scraps. It's a lighter-bodied soup, just right when served as an appetizer, maybe with a glass of Cabernet from Stellenbosch or the North Fork. If you like your soup a little heartier, just use less water. Either way, it's great topped with croutons (see page 72).

1 pound slab bacon, diced

2 medium yellow onions, chopped

1 cup fresh garlic cloves, roughly chopped

1 cup dry white wine

4 russet potatoes (about 4 pounds), peeled and quartered

1 head of roasted garlic (see page 235)

2 teaspoons kosher salt

¾ teaspoon freshly ground black pepper

1 TO MAKE THE SOUP: Combine the bacon, onions, and garlic in a large pot; cook over medium heat until the onions are translucent, about 10 minutes. Pour in the wine and increase the heat to high. Cook, scraping up any browned bits from the bottom of the pan, until the wine is reduced by one quarter, about 3 minutes.

2 Stir in the potatoes, roasted garlic, and 2 quarts water. Bring to a boil, reduce the heat to medium-high, and simmer until the potatoes are very tender, about 1 hour.

3 Let the soup cool slightly, then puree in batches in a food processor or blender (do not strain). The soup can be refrigerated, covered, for up to 3 days. Return the soup to the stove. Season with salt and pepper. Cook until heated through, about 5 minutes. Serve.

MARTHA'S EXCELLENT MATZOH BALL SOUP

SERVES 6 TO 8

Martha brought the matzoh balls" was often exclaimed with delight and relief at our family gatherings and holidays. It meant that even if the brisket was over-cooked and the blintzes dry, the kugel too sweet and the chopped liver bland, it would all fall away once you bit into one of those ethereal, cloudlike matzoh balls. Our grandmother Martha's influence is everywhere in this book and in our restaurants, but it is perhaps greatest in this dish, which epitomizes her grace in so many ways. Her matzoh balls walk the line between soft and firm. They hold their shape and don't fall apart when you cut them, but they melt in the mouth. The broth is pretty special, too, flecked with dill and dotted with golden puddles of schmaltz floating on the surface. Martha never let the matzoh balls sit in the broth, which makes the soup cloudy and overcooks the matzoh balls. Instead, she cooked them separately and then combined them with the broth just before serving.

CHICKEN BROTH

1 whole chicken (3 to 4 pounds)

1 tablespoon kosher salt

5 celery stalks with leaves, chopped

3 carrots, peeled and chopped

1 onion, chopped

3 garlic cloves, peeled

4 sprigs of fresh flat-leaf parsley

3 sprigs of fresh dill

½ teaspoon black peppercorns

2 dried bay leaves

MATZOH BALLS

4 large eggs

1 cup matzoh meal

2 tablespoons schmaltz (rendered chicken fat, reserved from making broth) or duck fat

1 tablespoon kosher salt

1 teaspoon baking powder

¼ cup seltzer water

3 carrots, peeled and sliced into ¼-inch-thick rounds (about 1 cup)

Salt and freshly ground black pepper

1½ tablespoons finely chopped fresh dill

| **TO MAKE THE BROTH:** Rub the chicken with the salt inside and out. Let rest on a plate in the refrigerator for 15 minutes. Rinse very well under cold running water and then pat dry with paper towels.

recipe continues

2   Put the chicken in a large stockpot and add enough cold water to cover by 3 inches. Bring to a boil, then skim off any foam that rises to the top. Add the celery, carrots, onion, garlic, parsley, dill, peppercorns, and bay leaves, and return the liquid to a boil. Skim again.

3   Reduce the heat and let simmer uncovered until the chicken is cooked, about 45 minutes. Transfer the chicken to a large bowl and, when cool enough to handle, take the meat off the bones (reserve the meat for another purpose; see Blue Ribbon Wisdom). Return the bones to the pot and simmer for 1 hour more. Strain through a cheesecloth-lined sieve, discarding the solids. Cool the broth slightly, then refrigerate until cold, overnight or up to 3 days.

4   Using a slotted spoon, skim off the solidified chicken fat from the broth. Save for making the matzoh balls or another purpose (see Blue Ribbon Wisdom).

5   TO MAKE THE MATZOH BALLS: In a large bowl, stir together the eggs, matzoh meal, schmaltz, salt, and baking powder. Add the seltzer and use a rubber spatula to mix well. Cover with plastic wrap and refrigerate for 1 hour.

6   Fill a large, wide pot (see Blue Ribbon Wisdom) with salted water and bring to a boil. Fill a small bowl with cold water and have nearby to keep your hands clean and wet. Working gently, without pressing, use clean, wet hands to form ½-inch-round matzoh balls. As they are formed, drop them into the boiling water. When all the matzoh balls are formed, cover the pot with a round of parchment paper to keep them submerged (or partially cover the pot with a lid if you don't have parchment paper) and simmer very gently (don't let the water boil again) until cooked through and tender, 45 minutes to 1 hour. Remove from the cooking liquid with a slotted spoon, and arrange in a single layer on a rimmed baking sheet. If not using that day, let cool to room temperature, then store the matzoh balls in a single layer in an airtight container filled with cooled cooking liquid to cover for up to 2 days.

7   To serve, gently heat the matzoh balls in a pot filled with matzoh ball cooking liquid or fresh water to cover (when the water comes to a simmer, taste a matzoh ball to see if it's hot enough, and either use immediately or continue to simmer until warmed to taste).

8 In a separate pot, bring the chicken broth to a boil. Add the carrot rounds and simmer until soft, about 7 minutes. Season to taste with salt and pepper, then add the dill.

9 Ladle the broth into individual serving bowls. Use a slotted spoon to transfer the warmed matzoh balls into the soup and serve piping hot.

blue ribbon wisdom

CHICKEN FAT Use the fat skimmed from the surface as a flavoring for soups, stews, sauces, and stir-fries. Just add a little bit to the oil or butter you're using to sauté the onions for the base.

A note on terminology: The fat skimmed from the top of the soup is not what our grandmother would consider to be proper schmaltz. To make true schmaltz, you need to cook onions in the chicken fat until they turn golden brown, then strain out the onions (our grandpa loved to eat them with steak or challah).

EVEN MORE ABOUT MATZOH BALLS To make matzoh balls that are light and fluffy all the way through without being rock hard in the center, it's imperative to let the batter rest in the fridge for an hour before cooking. This gives the matzoh meal time to absorb all the liquid and to relax, just like in a pie or bread dough.

Make sure you use a wide rather than tall pot so the matzoh balls fit in one even layer and have plenty of room to bob around. The matzoh balls are done when they rise to the surface and roll around evenly when you poke them.

MOM'S PERFECT CHICKEN SALAD This is a great way to use up that poached chicken you'll have after making this soup: Dice up the meat, and mix it with mayonnaise, salt, plenty of pepper, and some chopped green apple. It's sweet, tart, creamy, and awesome.

BLUE RIBBON HUMMUS

MAKES 2 SCANT CUPS

We've loved hummus ever since we first sampled it in the 1970s when we traveled to Israel for Eric's bar mitzvah. It kept us from driving our parents crazy with requests for grilled open-faced cheese and bologna sandwiches. It was probably one of the first recipes we learned to master at home when we were teenagers, and since then we have made it every which way, with canned chickpeas, cooked dried chickpeas, raw garlic, cooked garlic, different amounts of tahini, you name it. And we discovered that while all hummus is pretty good, this creamy, mild recipe and its garlicky variation are our favorites.

To avoid too much variation from batch to batch, we use canned chickpeas, which we think taste just as good as cooked dried peas. Another technique particular to us is cooking the garlic slightly for the garlic variation. Quickly cooking the garlic in a little oil smooths out and enhances the flavor. Make sure not to overcook the garlic. If it has browned all over, it will harden, and you won't be able to blend it with the chickpeas into a nice, velvety puree.

1 (15-ounce) can chickpeas, drained

¼ cup tahini

2 tablespoons freshly squeezed lemon juice, or to taste

½ teaspoon ground cumin

½ teaspoon Perfect Sauté Seasoning (page 251) or salt and freshly ground white or black pepper, or more to taste

Puree the chickpeas, tahini, lemon juice, cumin, and seasoning in a food processor until very smooth. Taste and add more lemon juice and seasoning if necessary.

VARIATION ▣ GARLICKY HUMMUS

Warm ¾ teaspoon minced garlic in 1½ tablespoons extra-virgin olive oil and pulse in the food processor before adding the rest of the hummus ingredients to combine.

GRILLED AND MARINATED CRUDITÉS

SERVES 4

All our lives growing up in New Jersey, we thought crudité meant carrot and celery sticks with a bowl of creamy dip. It was a real eye-opener on a trip to Provence with our parents in the 1980s to see crudité served as a mix of marinated and grilled vegetables with a light dressing.

We discovered a whole new way of eating, most of it taking place on the stone rooftop terrace of our sixteenth-century rental house. There was wine from the region—Vacqueyras, Gigondas, Châteauneuf-du-Pape—served with a variety of local goat's- and sheep's-milk cheeses. Sometimes there would be anchovy paste and olives, other days, country pâté and whole-grain mustard, always eaten with a crunchy baguette from the local bakery. But no matter what else we had, there were always fresh vegetables from the sun-drenched valley. This dish transports us straight back to that rooftop, and shows that the experience of cooking and eating, even something as simple as a plate of grilled vegetables, can be so much more than just sustenance.

2 small beets, trimmed

¼ pound asparagus, trimmed

¼ pound green beans, trimmed

2 medium leeks, white and light green parts only, halved lengthwise

1 fennel bulb, trimmed and cut lengthwise into ½-inch slabs

2 small heads of endive, quartered lengthwise

1 tablespoon extra-virgin olive oil

Perfect Sauté Seasoning (page 251) or salt and freshly ground white or black pepper

House Vinaigrette (page 244), for serving

1 Preheat the oven to 425°F.

2 Wrap the beets tightly in aluminum foil and place the foil packet on a rimmed baking sheet. Bake until the beets are fork tender, 45 minutes to 1 hour. Cool, then slip off the skins, and quarter the beets.

recipe continues

3 Meanwhile, bring a large pot of salted water to a boil. Fill a large bowl with water and ice. Add the asparagus to the boiling water and blanch until crisp-tender, 1 to 1½ minutes. Use a slotted spoon to transfer the asparagus to the ice water to stop the cooking; drain well.

4 Add more ice to the water bowl. Add the green beans to the boiling water and blanch until crisp-tender, 1 to 1½ minutes. Transfer the beans to the ice water; drain well. Set the vegetables aside.

5 Fill a large pot with 1 inch water and bring to a simmer. Clean the leeks under running water; do not separate the layers. Place the leeks in a steamer basket and steam the leeks, covered, until tender, 6 to 8 minutes. Remove the leeks and set aside. Replenish the water in the pot if it has evaporated, and return to a simmer. Steam the fennel in the basket, covered, until just tender, 4 to 5 minutes. Remove the fennel and set aside. Repeat with the endive until just tender, about 2 minutes.

6 Preheat a grill pan until very hot. In a bowl, toss the fennel and endive with the oil and seasoning. Grill the fennel and endive until lightly charred, 1 to 2 minutes per side. To serve, arrange the vegetables on a platter and drizzle lightly with the dressing.

ROASTED GARLIC CAESAR SALAD

When you order a Caesar salad made with real Parmigiano-Reggiano, the good stuff, the dressing has little grains in it from the aged cheese. And that's okay, but we wanted something creamier. So we started making a silky smooth paste of Parmesan and oil by "cooking" the cheese and oil in our heavy-duty professional food processor. Basically, we'd let the cheese and oil mixture run in the machine until it generated enough heat to slightly melt the cheese so it emulsifies with the oil. (In a home kitchen, we recommend heating the oil until barely warm to the touch and then processing it with the cheese.)

Roasting the garlic gives our Caesar dressing a mellow and slightly sweet flavor, but if you want more of a garlicky punch, feel free to add some raw minced garlic to the food processor along with the other ingredients. Or, if you're using a wooden salad bowl, rub a cut garlic clove all over the inside surface before tossing the salad. It will give you just a hint of raw garlic without the risk of overkill.

CROUTONS

3½ cups cubed day-old peasant bread

2½ tablespoons roasted garlic oil (page 235)

2 tablespoons grated Parmigiano-Reggiano cheese

Perfect Sauté Seasoning (page 251) or salt and freshly ground white or black pepper

DRESSING

¾ teaspoon chopped shallots

1 tablespoon dry white wine

6 tablespoons extra-virgin olive oil

6 tablespoons freshly grated Parmigiano-Reggiano cheese

2 large egg yolks

1 large egg

¼ cup Anchovy Paste (page 241)

¼ cup freshly squeezed lemon juice

2 tablespoons Roasted Garlic Puree (page 235)

1 teaspoon finely chopped garlic (optional; see headnote)

Freshly ground black pepper

Salt, if needed

3 hearts of romaine (the pale, light-colored centers only), torn into large pieces

| **TO MAKE THE CROUTONS:** Preheat the oven to 350°F.

2   In a large bowl, toss the bread, garlic oil, and cheese together and add season-
    ing to taste. Spread the croutons on a rimmed baking sheet and bake, tossing
    halfway through, until dry and golden, about 20 minutes. Let cool. The crou-
    tons will keep in an airtight container at room temperature for up to 2 weeks.

3   TO MAKE THE DRESSING: In a small bowl combine the shallots and wine; let sit for
    10 minutes to allow the intensity of the shallots to mellow.

4   Pour the olive oil in a small saucepan and cook over medium heat until warm
    to the touch (about 110°F), not hot.

5   Put the cheese in the bowl of a food processor fitted with the blade attachment.
    With the motor running, slowly drizzle in the warm oil. Let run until a smooth,
    homogenous paste forms, 5 to 10 minutes. With the motor still running, add
    the egg yolks and egg, blend until smooth, and then blend in the anchovy paste,
    lemon juice, roasted and fresh garlic, shallots and wine, and pepper. Taste and
    adjust the seasoning, adding salt, if necessary.

6   In a salad bowl, toss the lettuce with the dressing to lightly coat. Add the
    croutons and drizzle with a little more dressing. Serve immediately.

blue ribbon wisdom

USING ROASTED GARLIC AND GARLIC OIL   We love roasted
garlic, which, packed in oil, will last up to a month in the fridge. If the
oil congeals on the top, that's okay; just scoop out the garlic you
need. The oil will return to liquid form at room temperature.

The oil surrounding the garlic (page 235) is fantastic to have on
hand, too. Here are some of our favorite ways to use it:
- Mix it into mashed potatoes.
- Mix it into store-bought mayo; people will think it's homemade aioli.
- Make a vinaigrette with red wine vinegar, salt, and pepper.
- Brush it on toasted bread for garlicky crostini (you can even break
  toasts into pieces for instant croutons).
- Drizzle it over fish or chicken, either before or after cooking.

BABY ARUGULA AND BUTTERNUT SQUASH SALAD
WITH MANCHEGO AND BALSAMIC VINAIGRETTE

SERVES 4

Combining soft roasted vegetables, spicy arugula, salty cheese, and a slightly sweet balsamic vinaigrette does great things for salad. We serve this at the wine bar, where it pairs perfectly with dry sherry or crisp white rioja, which plays off the manchego for a distinctly Spanish tapas vibe.

1 medium butternut squash, peeled and halved lengthwise, seeds removed

7 tablespoons extra-virgin olive oil

1 tablespoon freshly squeezed orange juice

2 tablespoons balsamic vinegar

Salt and freshly ground black pepper

8 cups baby arugula

2 ounces manchego cheese, very thinly sliced

1 Preheat the oven to 375°F.

2 Place the squash, cut side up, on a foil-lined rimmed baking sheet. Drizzle with 1 tablespoon of the oil. Roast until very tender, about 1 hour. Let cool completely, then cut into ½-inch cubes.

3 TO MAKE THE VINAIGRETTE: Whisk together the orange juice, vinegar, and a pinch of salt. Slowly drizzle in the remaining 6 tablespoons of the oil, whisking constantly, until completely incorporated.

4 To assemble, divide the squash among serving plates (about 1 cup per serving). Sprinkle lightly with salt and pepper. Divide the arugula among the plates. Top each salad with cheese slices, drizzle each salad with some of the vinaigrette (reserve any remaining vinaigrette for another use), and serve.

MARKET SALAD

It's not often that Bob's Big Boy is cited for culinary inspiration. But so it was on a road trip to Florida back in 1997—before the Blue Ribbon Bakery opened—with our buddy and partner Sefton Stallard. Now the trip from New York to Florida does hold its fair share of culinary hotbeds such as Yamasee, Savannah, and the Chesapeake Bay area, but one particularly barren stretch of nondescript scenery between Washington and one of the Virginias held little promise in terms of lunch, other than fast-food joints: Burger King, 11 miles ahead; Arby's, 14 miles ahead; then HoJo's.

Suddenly, there it was, a glorious brick-red sign: BOB'S BIG BOY, NEXT EXIT.

"I think they actually cook there," Sefton said.

"Like vegetables and stuff?" we wondered.

"Look, it says it's a family restaurant. Let's do it!"

Once we settled into the plastic seats, Bob's signature salad hit the table: string beans, chickpeas, onions, hard-boiled eggs, asparagus, olives, crunchy romaine, and a creamy mustard sauce . . . perfect. And perfect to serve a variation of it at Blue Ribbon Bakery when it opened. This salad is unquestionably the most popular salad on any of our menus to date, and you know, we've never properly thanked Bob. So thanks, Bob, whoever you are!

1 medium beet, trimmed

4 large eggs

8 asparagus stalks

4 cups chopped romaine lettuce (from about 2 heads)

1 carrot, peeled and grated (1 cup)

1 tomato, chopped (1 cup)

1 English cucumber, peeled, seeded, and cubed (¾ cup)

¾ cup chopped kalamata olives

¾ cup chopped Grilled Red Onions (page 232)

4 marinated artichoke hearts

House Vinaigrette (page 244)

Chopped fresh chives, for garnish

1   Preheat the oven to 425°F.

2   Wrap the beet tightly in aluminum foil and place the foil packet on a rimmed baking sheet. Bake until the beet is fork tender, about 1 hour. Cool, then slip off the skin, and cut the beet into cubes.

3   Meanwhile, place the eggs in a medium pot and fill with water to cover by 1 inch; bring the water to a boil. Immediately turn off the heat. Cover the pot for 3 minutes. Uncover and let the eggs cool in the water. Peel and halve lengthwise.

4   Bring a large pot of salted water to a boil. Fill a large bowl with water and ice. Boil the asparagus until crisp-tender, 1 to 1½ minutes. Plunge immediately in the ice water; drain well.

5   Divide the romaine among 4 dinner plates. Scatter the beets, carrot, tomato, cucumber, olives, and onions over the romaine (like a pizza pie). Cross two asparagus stalks over the top of each salad. Top each with two egg halves and a marinated artichoke heart. Drizzle with vinaigrette and garnish with chives. Serve immediately.

SMOKED TROUT SALAD
WITH GRANNY SMITH APPLE, ENDIVE, WATERCRESS, AND CREAMY DILL DRESSING

SERVES 6 TO 8

Smoked trout is something we've loved ever since our dad took us fishing up in northern Manitoba, polar bear country, about 100 miles south of Hudson Bay. Trout were plentiful up there, and we'd reel them in one after another. Then after a long day on the boat, we'd head back to the lodge where the owners, Doug and Helen Webber, would have a platter of smoked trout canapés waiting for us. When we got our own smoker at Blue Ribbon, it seemed obvious to start with trout fillets. We love the intense, savory flavor. It's a little bit subtler than smoked salmon, and the flaky texture works really well in this salad with the sweetness of the crisp green apple and the creamy dill dressing.

½ cup House Vinaigrette (page 244)

¼ cup sour cream

2 tablespoons chopped fresh dill

1 medium beet, trimmed

4½ cups watercress

3 cups mixed salad greens

3 cups chopped endive (from about 6 endives)

4 ounces smoked trout, flaked

1 medium Granny Smith apple, cored and chopped

1 Whisk together the vinaigrette, sour cream, and dill with 2 tablespoons water. Cover the dressing and refrigerate until ready to use (up to 3 days).

2 Preheat the oven to 425°F.

3 Wrap the beet tightly in aluminum foil and place the foil packet on a rimmed baking sheet. Bake until the beet is fork tender, about 1 hour. Cool, then slip off the skin, and cut the beet into cubes.

4 In a large bowl, combine the beet with the watercress, salad greens, endive, trout, and apple and toss well. Add just enough of the dressing to lightly coat the greens. Toss again before serving.

main dishes

◉ beef marrow bones with oxtail marmalade ◉ hanger steak with caramelized onions, mushrooms, and pan-roasted potatoes ◉ really good brisket ◉ new york strip steak with caramelized shallots ◉ braised beef short ribs with succotash ◉ rack of lamb with thyme and roasted tomato sauce ◉ crispy cornish hens ◉ northern fried chicken ◉ herb-roasted chicken with lemon and sage ◉ seared long island duck breast with orange-cassis sauce ◉ shrimp provençal with pernod ◉ grilled salmon with mustard sauce ◉ grilled red trout with string beans, bacon, and almonds ◉ roasted striped bass with red wine sauce ◉ paella basquez

The main dish is the heart of the meal and always gets the most attention. Entire holidays are centered around the main: what would Thanksgiving be without turkey, Easter without lamb, or the Fourth of July without hamburgers and hot dogs? And even on any old day, the main is pretty important. Whether you rushed home after soccer practice for your favorite pot roast or tried to miss the bus when you knew it was liver and onions night, it's always the main dish that matters most.

We find more and more that we dine at restaurants that have great, inventive appetizers, but then the main is somehow disappointing. Remember that it doesn't really matter how delectable the sauce or the sides are if the main item is overcooked or lacking in flavor. Always invest some time and lots of love in your main dish, as it's what has brought everybody to the table.

Growing up, everybody has a favorite or two. One of ours was roasted chicken, which we still serve, a little gussied up as Herb-Roasted Chicken with Lemon and Sage (page 101). And we loved the steamed flounder Dad would order for us on our Chinatown excursions.

Then there were some dishes we loved, but knew we could make just that much better. We became fixated on making ultimate versions of almost-favorites and the result is our Braised Beef Short Ribs with Succotash (page 92) and Northern Fried Chicken (page 98). Of all the mains in this chapter, those two really highlight the spirit of what we're trying to do at Blue Ribbon—that is, create the best possible recipes of dishes everyone thinks they know how to make well enough. We like to shake things up in our quest for perfection, and the proof is in the pudding—or in the Hanger Steak with Caramelized Onions, Mushrooms, and Pan-Roasted Potatoes (page 87), as the case may be.

BEEF MARROW BONES
WITH OXTAIL MARMALADE

There's one dish that has defined Blue Ribbon over the past seventeen years, and it's nothing more than a platter of bones. But what bones! We scrape them clean until pristine white and filled with glistening, near-liquid sumptuous marrow, and we serve them surrounded by sweet and savory oxtail marmalade, warm toasted challah bread, and a pile of coarse sea salt. Each bite is slightly different as the proportions of ingredients vary, but we think that makes it even more sublime.

There was a time when we had to beg and plead to get our butcher to send us the bones cut just so. They didn't seem to understand that the bones were meant for diners, not for the stockpot. In fairness, marrow bones serve many different purposes, so make sure you tell your butcher exactly how you'll be using yours.

MARROW BONES

3 pounds center-cut beef marrow bones cut into 2-inch pieces, tendons trimmed (ask your butcher to do this)

¼ cup kosher salt, plus more if needed

OXTAIL MARMALADE

4 pounds oxtail, trimmed of fat

6 cups port wine

6 cups dry red wine

4 quarts veal or chicken stock, homemade (pages 248 and 247) or purchased

1 head of garlic, halved crosswise

½ bunch of fresh thyme

1 tablespoon black peppercorns

8 tablespoons (1 stick) unsalted butter

3 tablespoons all-purpose flour

1½ pounds carrots, peeled, trimmed, and cut into ¼-inch cubes (about 4 cups)

1 pound shallots, peeled and cut into ¼-inch cubes (about 4 cups)

1½ teaspoons kosher salt, plus more to taste

½ cup granulated sugar

½ cup (packed) light brown sugar

1 cup red wine vinegar

2½ teaspoons freshly ground black pepper, plus more to taste

3 slices challah bread, homemade (page 200) or you favorite store-bought soft loaf, toasted and still warm, cut into quarters

Chopped fresh flat-leaf parsley leaves, for serving

Fleur de sel or other good-quality coarse sea salt, for serving

recipe continues

1   TO SOAK THE MARROW BONES: Place the bones in a large bowl. Combine the salt with 4 cups cold water; pour over the bones. If the water does not cover the bones, add a solution of 1 cup water to 1 tablespoon salt at a time, until the bones are covered. Soak in the refrigerator for 36 to 48 hours, changing the water three times, until the bones are bleached of color. Drain well.

2   TO MAKE THE MARMALADE: Combine the oxtail, 3 cups of the port, the red wine, veal stock, garlic, thyme, and peppercorns in a large pot. Bring the mixture to a boil, reduce the heat, and simmer for 3 hours.

3   Transfer the oxtail to a bowl; when cool enough to handle, remove the meat from the bones and cut it into small cubes. Refrigerate the meat until ready to use. Strain the oxtail liquid into a large skillet, discarding the solids. Bring the liquid to a boil over high heat; reduce the heat to medium and simmer until the mixture is reduced to 3 cups, 1½ to 2 hours.

4   While it reduces, combine 3 tablespoons of the butter with the flour until it forms a paste. Whisk the paste, 1 tablespoon at a time, into the reduced liquid over medium heat. Cook until the mixture thickens slightly, about 3 minutes.

5   In a separate large skillet, melt the remaining 5 tablespoons butter. Add the carrots, shallots, and a pinch of salt over medium heat until slightly softened, about 15 minutes. Stir in the sugars, the remaining 3 cups port, the vinegar, the 1½ teaspoons salt, and 1½ teaspoons of the pepper. Cook over medium-high heat until the liquid has completely evaporated, about 45 minutes. Stir in the oxtail meat, thickened oxtail cooking liquid, and remaining 1 teaspoon pepper. Taste and adjust the seasonings if necessary. Set aside or transfer the marmalade to an airtight container and refrigerate overnight. (Before serving, reheat in a saucepan over medium heat until warmed through.)

6   TO COOK THE MARROW BONES: Place the bones in a large saucepan and cover with water. Bring to a simmer over medium heat (do not let the water come to a boil or the marrow will melt out of the bones). To test for doneness, place a thin metal knife in the center of the marrow and hold it under your lip to see if it's hot. When hot, remove the bones from the water and drain well.

7   Arrange the bones and challah toasts on the platter. Spoon oxtail marmalade in between the bones (reserve remaining marmalade for another use). Sprinkle with chopped parsley and coarse sea salt.

HANGER STEAK
WITH CARAMELIZED ONIONS, MUSHROOMS, AND PAN-ROASTED POTATOES

SERVES 4

This recipe combines flavors from two of our all-time favorite restaurants: Benihana in Short Hills, New Jersey, and Le Recamier in Paris.

While hanger steak is just starting to really gain a cult following here, it's always had a place on menus across Europe as an affordable, meaty, flavorful cut of beef. In France, seared *onglet* is usually slathered in buttery, brown, slow-cooked shallots and hidden beneath a jumble of slender, crispy, perfectly salted fries. To mess with this combination of flavors and textures would be considered a heinous act across the Atlantic. But in the States we have more flexibility with the garnishes.

And that's where Benihana fits in. When we went to Benihana as kids, we always ordered zucchini and onions, which we loved to watch the chefs prepare tableside at super-fast speed. In our version we use mushrooms in place of the zucchini, but combined with the lightly browned onions, they bring back happy Benihana memories. If you'd like a more Parisian experience, feel free to garnish the steak with Shallot Confit (page 235) and French Fries (page 121) instead of the mushrooms and pan-roasted potatoes.

POTATOES

1½ pounds medium white potatoes, scrubbed

2 tablespoons unsalted butter

1½ tablespoons olive oil

3 tablespoons chopped fresh flat-leaf parsley leaves

Perfect Sauté Seasoning (page 251) or salt and freshly ground black pepper

MUSHROOMS AND ONIONS

3 tablespoons unsalted butter

2 onions, sliced into ½-inch-thick rings

¾ pound cremini mushrooms, wiped clean, trimmed, and sliced

Perfect Sauté Seasoning (page 251) or salt and freshly ground white or black pepper

3 tablespoons chopped fresh flat-leaf parsley leaves (optional)

STEAK

2 teaspoons olive oil

4 (7-ounce) hanger steaks

Perfect Sauté Seasoning (page 251) or salt and freshly ground white or black pepper

recipe continues

1   To make the potatoes: Put the potatoes in a large pot and add salted water to cover. Bring to a boil. Cook the potatoes until just barely tender, 20 to 25 minutes. Drain and cool. Slice the potatoes into ¼-inch-thick matchsticks.

2   Preheat the oven to 450°F.

3   To crisp the potatoes, in a large skillet over medium heat, heat 1 tablespoon of the butter with the oil. Add the potatoes to the hot skillet and cook, tossing occasionally, until golden brown all over, about 10 minutes. Toss the potatoes with the remaining 1 tablespoon butter, the parsley, and the seasoning. Cover to keep warm, or transfer to a platter and tent with foil.

4   Meanwhile, prepare the mushrooms and onions: In a skillet over medium-high heat, melt the butter. Add the onions and cook, stirring occasionally, until softened and translucent, 3 to 5 minutes. Add the mushrooms and cook, stirring, until they are browned and tender, 7 to 8 minutes. Sprinkle with seasoning and parsley, if using, and cover to keep warm.

5   To cook the steak: Heat the oil in a cast-iron pan over high heat until very, very hot, at least 5 solid minutes. Sprinkle the steaks all over with the seasoning. Sear the steaks in the pan until well browned on all sides, about 2 minutes per side. Transfer the steaks to the oven and roast until desired doneness is reached, about 3 more minutes for rare (115°F on an instant-read thermometer) and 5 for medium-rare (120°F on an instant-read thermometer). Transfer to serving plates, tent with foil, and let rest for at least 3 minutes before serving with the potatoes, mushrooms, and onions.

blue ribbon wisdom

HOT PAN FOR LEAN CUTS Kris Polak, our chef-partner and spiritual consigliere, has seared more hanger steaks than almost anyone on this planet. He says you have to sear very lean cuts like hanger steak in a *hot* pan so you don't end up steaming the meat in its own juices rather than searing it. Do not overcook hanger steak; take it off the heat just before it's done to your taste, then let it rest for a few minutes to finish cooking.

REALLY GOOD BRISKET

After many, many years of having brisket as the centerpiece of family holiday meals, it was a personal quest for us to come up with our own exceptional brisket recipe. This may come as a surprise to you, but brisket doesn't need to be a dried-out stringy mess. One thing that we particularly loved about our mom's brisket is the pureed vegetable sauce served on top of the meat. Instead of straining out the aromatic vegetables from the pot as a chef would traditionally do, we just leave it all in there and puree everything that's in the pan. You'll end up with an incredibly rich, full-bodied, and luscious sauce. Another fun trick we've added is using onions on the bottom of the pot in place of a rack; it's an easy way to add flavor.

1 (3- to 3½-pound) brisket

Perfect Roast Seasoning (page 251) or kosher salt and freshly ground black pepper

4 tablespoons (½ stick) unsalted butter

5 pounds (about 10) small yellow onions, peeled and halved through the root

1 cup dry white wine

1 cup veal or chicken stock, homemade (pages 248 and 247) or purchased, or more if needed

1½ tablespoons fresh thyme leaves

1 teaspoon freshly ground black pepper

2 celery stalks, diced

1 tomato, diced

4 garlic cloves, peeled

1 Preheat the oven to 300°F.

2 Sprinkle the brisket with the seasoning and let stand for 15 minutes. Melt the butter in the bottom of a Dutch oven. Arrange the onions, cut side down, in the pot. Cook over medium heat for about 7 minutes, until well browned on the bottom. Pour the wine and stock over the onions, covering them by 1 inch. Add more stock, if necessary. Add the thyme and pepper. Bring the liquid to a simmer on the stovetop. Place the brisket, fatty side up, on top of the onions. Sprinkle the celery, tomato, and garlic over the brisket. Cover and cook in the oven, turning once, until very tender, about 3½ hours.

3 Transfer the brisket to a serving platter and boil the braising liquid over high heat until reduced by half, about 15 minutes. Puree the liquid and vegetables in a food processor and then strain through a fine-mesh sieve. Serve the sauce alongside.

NEW YORK STRIP STEAK
WITH CARAMELIZED SHALLOTS

SERVES 4

We call New York strip steak "the benchmark." It is one of the most simple and straightforward American dishes to prepare, and because of that, it's a way to judge if a restaurant is on the ball or not. When properly cooked on the grill or some other source of high heat, a strip steak is a unique combination of buttery tenderness, a charred surface, and a rare center that oozes tasty fat. We think it's the only piece of beef to go for when you're really in the mood for steak. A strip steak doesn't even need a sauce; we serve ours smothered with buttery caramelized shallots to add a little sweetness and round out the meat. But even served naked, if you cook it right, you can't go wrong.

CARAMELIZED SHALLOTS	STEAK
6 tablespoons unsalted butter	4 (12-ounce) New York strip steaks
1 pound shallots, trimmed and thinly sliced	Olive oil
	Perfect Sauté Seasoning (page 251) or salt and freshly ground white or black pepper

1 TO COOK THE SHALLOTS: Melt the butter in a large skillet over medium heat. Add the shallots and reduce the heat to low. Cook, stirring occasionally, until the shallots are dark amber (but not burned), about 30 minutes. You can make these up to 1 week ahead and store in the fridge. Bring them up to room temperature before serving.

2 TO COOK THE STEAK: Preheat a grill or grill pan until very hot. Coat the steaks with oil and season generously all over. Sear, without moving, until a dark golden crust forms, 4 to 5 minutes. Flip the steaks and cook until the desired temperature is reached, 4 to 5 minutes more for medium-rare (120°F on an instant-read thermometer). Let the steaks stand for 5 minutes before serving, topped with the shallots.

BRAISED BEEF SHORT RIBS
WITH SUCCOTASH

SERVES 4

This incredible dish by our partner and buddy chef Sefton Stallard has kept folks flocking to the Blue Ribbon Bakery on cold winter nights for years and years. Their objective? To get a seat near the cozy warmth of the 140-year-old brick oven and savor a big bowl of some "Seftonian" delight just like this one. Short ribs are a cut of meat that just loves red wine and a long slow cooking time in a covered pot. When the ribs emerge, they are soft and juicy, bursting with mellow hints of tannic wine, sweet vegetables, black pepper, and plenty of garlic. The lima beans and corn in the succotash are heightened by a corn stock that gives body and elegance to the dish, while spicy, fresh arugula added at the end provides a nice bite.

SHORT RIBS

2½ pounds short ribs (about 10)

Perfect Roast Seasoning (page 250) or kosher salt and freshly ground black pepper

½ cup extra-virgin olive oil

1 onion, diced

1 head of garlic, cloves separated and peeled

1 leek, trimmed and halved crosswise

1 carrot, peeled, trimmed, and halved crosswise

1 bay leaf

1 teaspoon black peppercorns

2 cups port wine

2 cups dry red wine

About 2 cups veal or chicken stock, homemade (pages 248 and 247) or purchased

SUCCOTASH

1 pound (2 cups) shelled fresh fava or lima beans

4 ears of corn, husked

2 tablespoons unsalted butter

1 onion, very finely chopped

Perfect Sauté Seasoning (page 251) or salt and freshly ground white or black pepper

2 cups (packed) arugula leaves, coarsely chopped

TO MAKE THE SHORT RIBS: Sprinkle the ribs with the seasoning. Heat the oil in a large Dutch oven over medium-high heat. Sear the ribs in two batches, turning once, for about 8 minutes or until golden. Transfer the ribs to a plate. Add the onion, garlic, leek, carrot, bay leaf, and peppercorns to the Dutch oven. Cook, stirring occasionally, for 5 to 7 minutes, until slightly softened. Add the port and red wine and bring to a boil. Let boil, scraping up the brown bits, for about 25 minutes, until the liquid has reduced by half.

2   Return the ribs to the pot and add enough stock to come halfway up the sides of the pot. Cover and reduce the heat to medium-low. Cook for about 2½ hours, until the meat is falling off the bone and shreds easily with a fork. Transfer the ribs to a platter. Reduce the sauce by half over high heat, about 15 minutes, and then strain, discarding the solids.

3   TO MAKE THE SUCCOTASH: Have a bowl of ice water ready to use as an ice bath. Blanch the fava beans in boiling salted water for 3 minutes or until tender. Immediately plunge them into the ice water to stop cooking.

4   Slice the kernels from the ears of corn and set the kernels aside. Combine the corncobs in a saucepan with 3 cups water and bring to a boil. Simmer until the liquid has reduced by two thirds. Add the fava beans and simmer for 2 to 3 minutes. Using a slotted spoon, transfer the beans to a small bowl. Discard the corncobs and reserve the remaining cooking liquid.

5   Melt the butter in a large skillet over medium-high heat. Add the onion and cook for about 5 minutes, until slightly caramelized. Reduce the heat to medium and add the corn kernels and ¼ cup of the cooking liquid. Cook, stirring occasionally, for 3 minutes. Add the beans and cook, stirring for 1 minute. Season the succotash and then stir in the arugula, tossing to wilt the leaves.

6   Spoon the succotash in the center of 4 plates. Divide the short ribs among the plates on top of the succotash. Spoon the sauce over the meat and serve.

blue ribbon wisdom

PEELING FAVA AND LIMA BEANS Some chefs peel lima and fava beans as a matter of course. We say, take a look at your beans. If they are young and tender with thin skins, you don't have to peel them. But if the skins are tough, after blanching the beans, use a paring knife or your fingers to slip off the skins.

RACK OF LAMB
WITH THYME AND ROASTED TOMATO SAUCE

SERVES 4 TO 6

Ever since our first rack-of-lamb experience at a now defunct San Francisco restaurant called Ernie's, where they sliced the meat tableside, we've been in love with the cut. A glorious combination of tender meat and flavorful fat enables lamb to stand up to so many wonderful flavors. Rosemary, mint, thyme, cumin, and curry are just a few. In this recipe we combine sweet shallot, red wine, and vibrant roasted tomatoes to create a rich sauce that is easy to make ahead and perfectly complements the richness and juiciness of the meat. Although most people think of lamb as special-occasion or holiday food, it's also a nice dish to whip up for a quiet night at home after the kids have gone to bed. And reason enough to open a nice bottle of wine.

ROASTED TOMATO SAUCE

2½ tablespoons unsalted butter, chilled and cut into small cubes

2 teaspoons finely chopped shallot

½ cup port wine

½ cup dry red wine

2 cups veal or chicken stock, homemade (pages 248 and 247) or purchased

½ cup chopped Roasted Tomatoes (page 230)

1½ teaspoons chopped fresh thyme leaves

LAMB

2 (8-rib, 1½-pound) frenched racks of lamb, trimmed of fat

1 tablespoon Perfect Roast Seasoning (page 250) or kosher salt and freshly ground black pepper

1   Preheat the oven to 450°F.

2   **TO MAKE THE SAUCE:** Melt ½ tablespoon of the butter in a nonreactive skillet over medium heat. Add the shallot and cook, stirring, until translucent, about 3 minutes. Add the port and red wine, increase the heat to high, and boil until the mixture has reduced to ½ cup, about 5 minutes. Stir in the stock and cook until the mixture has reduced to almost ¾ cup, 5 to 7 minutes more. Stir in the tomatoes and thyme. Remove from the heat. You can make the sauce up to 1 week ahead and refrigerate.

recipe continues

3 Sprinkle the lamb generously all over with the seasoning. Heat a large, heavy-bottomed ovenproof skillet over high heat until hot but not smoking. Add the lamb, bone side up; reduce the heat to medium-high and sear the lamb until golden brown, about 10 minutes. Do not turn the racks. Pour off any excess fat.

4 Transfer the pan to the oven. Cook until the fat is fully rendered, about 5 minutes. Turn the rack and cook to desired doneness, 5 to 10 minutes more for medium-rare (120°F on an instant-read thermometer). Transfer the meat to a cutting board to rest for 15 minutes before slicing between the bones.

5 While the meat rests, reheat the sauce over low heat. Whisk in the remaining 2 tablespoons of butter, a few cubes at a time, until thoroughly incorporated. Transfer the lamb chops to serving plates. Drizzle with the sauce and serve.

blue ribbon wisdom

CARAMELIZING ONIONS AND SHALLOTS Home cooks sometimes skip recipes that call for caramelizing onions and shallots thinking it'll be too complicated or time consuming—which is a real shame because there is nothing like the deep salty-sweetness they impart. We offer a few pointers with an eye toward keeping it simple.

- Don't season your onions or shallots at all before or during cooking. The salt will cause them to release too much liquid too fast.
- Keep the temperature a constant medium. If the pan gets too hot, the onions and shallots will brown unevenly and burn in spots, making them bitter. But if the pan isn't hot enough, it can take hours for the onions to caramelize.
- Cover the pan. As the onions and shallots cook they let off steam, which is captured by the cover. The steam drips back down into the pan and softens the onions, keeping them from getting too dark but allowing them to melt and sweeten.
- Occasionally (but not constantly), check your onions and shallots and give them a stir. With the cover on, there's no need to waste time hovering over the stove; you can go do something else. They won't burn, and you'll get perfect caramelization without much fuss.

CRISPY CORNISH HENS

SERVES 4

The best part about this dish is the amazingly crunchy skin that the hens get from being butterflied and then laid flat in a very hot pan. Unlike a roasted, whole Cornish hen, every part of the bird gets a chance to crisp up because all the skin comes in contact with the sizzling skillet. The legs, the thighs, the breasts, the wings, everything becomes wonderfully golden and crispy. It's a technique we learned in France that is usually applied to smaller birds—pigeons and quails and the like. Not only does it cook the birds really nicely, it makes them easy to eat since you can really get at everything. We thought that it would work well with Cornish hens, which are like the bigger, fatter, American equivalent to all those little French birds, and we love to serve them with our Creamy Mashed Potatoes (page 122).

4 (1½-pound) Cornish hens	6 tablespoons sugar
¾ cup kosher salt	2½ tablespoons extra-virgin olive oil

1 Rinse the hens inside and out. Using kitchen shears, cut along each side of one hen's backbone (tail to neck) and remove. Grasp each side of the hen's ribcage and pull the carcass open until you hear a crack. Repeat with the remaining hens. (Or have your butcher butterfly them for you.)

2 In a large bowl or stockpot, stir together 9 cups water with the salt and sugar until dissolved. Place the hens in the brine. Cover and refrigerate for 1½ hours.

3 Preheat the oven to 475°F.

4 Remove the hens from the brine and pat completely dry. Heat a large oven-proof skillet (or two skillets if the hens won't fit into one) over medium-high heat until very hot, but not smoking. Toss the hens with the oil and then arrange in the skillet, skin side down. Try to keep them as flat as possible while cooking. Cook, without moving, until the skin is brown and crispy, about 10 minutes. Flip the birds and transfer the skillet to the oven. Continue to cook until an instant-read thermometer inserted in the thickest part of the thigh registers 145°F, about 6 minutes more. Turn the birds and continue roasting until the temperature reaches 160°F, 2 to 3 minutes longer. Remove the hens from the oven and let rest for several minutes before serving.

NORTHERN FRIED CHICKEN

SERVES 4

So how did a couple of Jewish guys from Jersey, who ventured to France to study at the most celebrated cooking school in the world, end up making a reputation for themselves based on finger-lickin'-good fried chicken? The answer: matzoh meal, which makes the chicken skin extra crisp without weighing it down or absorbing too much oil.

Then to add even more flavor, after cooking, we sprinkle the chicken pieces with our special fried chicken spices and serve them with our good Mexican honey for dipping. It's a dish that embodies the guiding philosophy of Blue Ribbon, which is to be a restaurant that people could eat at every day, and to make the best versions possible of lovable classics. You can say it's better than home cooking.

6 cups soy oil

1 (3-pound) chicken, cut into 8 pieces (2 legs, 2 thighs, 4 breast pieces)

4 large egg whites, whisked

½ cup matzoh meal

½ cup all-purpose flour

¼ teaspoon baking powder

Perfect Sauté Seasoning (page 251) or salt and freshly ground white or black pepper

1 teaspoon Fried Chicken Seasoning (page 251)

Chicken Gravy (page 249), for serving (optional)

Mexican honey, for serving

1   Fill a large pot with about 3 inches of oil. Heat the oil over medium-high heat until a deep-fat thermometer reads 375°F.

2   Rinse the chicken pieces and pat dry with paper towels. Place the egg whites in a large shallow bowl. In a separate shallow bowl, combine the matzoh meal, flour, and baking powder. Dip each chicken piece in egg white and let excess drip back into the bowl. Next press each chicken piece into the matzoh mix and tap off excess.

3   Working in 2 batches, if necessary, fry the chicken until dark golden, about 10 minutes for white meat and 13 minutes for dark meat. Transfer to a paper-towel-lined plate. Sprinkle immediately with the perfect sauté seasoning, then coat the pieces with the fried chicken seasoning. Serve with gravy if you like, and honey, for dipping.

HERB-ROASTED CHICKEN
WITH LEMON AND SAGE

SERVES 4

We hit upon our favorite recipe a few summers back, when we helped out a buddy with his annual Labor Day pig roast in Connecticut. In addition to the 125-pound porker we were planning to serve, we decided we should have some chicken just in case not everyone at the party wanted to partake of the sacred swine. We got about 100 birds, halved them, and soaked them in a simple marinade of just lemon, sage, and cracked black pepper. It turned out to be one of the first times—maybe the only time—there was a pig roast where chicken was the hit of the day. What really made it special was the marinade. It lent a nice acidity to the meat, which became really tender, and the sage and lemon flavors just exploded.

For the most classic presentation, roast a whole bird and carve it tableside. If you want an especially crispy, golden-skinned chicken, have your butcher halve it, and roast the halves skin side up so they can self-baste as they roast.

1 (3- to 3½-pound) whole chicken, patted dry with paper towels

½ cup extra-virgin olive oil

1 lemon, thinly sliced

1 bunch of fresh sage leaves (about ½ cup)

2 teaspoons Perfect Roast Seasoning (page 250) or kosher salt and freshly ground black pepper

3 medium carrots, peeled and halved crosswise (for whole chicken only), optional

3 celery stalks, cut crosswise into thirds (for whole chicken only), optional

1 large onion, peeled and cut into large chunks (for whole chicken only), optional

FOR A WHOLE CHICKEN

1 Put the chicken in a large bowl. Add the oil, lemon, and sage; toss well. Cover tightly and transfer to the refrigerator to marinate for 24 hours.

2 The next day, let the chicken stand at room temperature for 30 minutes while the oven preheats to 450°F.

3 Sprinkle the chicken inside and out with the seasoning. Remove the lemon slices and sage from the marinade and stuff them inside the chicken cavity.

recipe continues

Scatter the carrots, celery, and onion, if using, over the bottom of a roasting pan. Pour just enough water into the pan to cover the bottom. Arrange the chicken, breast side up, on top of the vegetables, if desired, or place the chicken on a roasting rack over the vegetables.

4 Transfer the pan to the center oven rack; roast for 20 minutes. Baste with the pan juices, and continue roasting, basting once or twice, for 25 minutes more (if the chicken is not golden brown all over at this point, continue to cook for 10 more minutes).

5 Reduce the heat to 325°F. Finish roasting, without basting, until an instant-read thermometer inserted in the thickest part of the thigh reads 165°F, 20 to 25 minutes longer. Let the chicken stand for 5 minutes before carving. Serve with the pan juices and vegetables, if desired.

FOR CHICKEN HALVES

1 Using kitchen shears, cut the chicken along each side of the backbone; remove the bone and discard. Cut the chicken in half along the breastbone and place in a large bowl. Add the oil, lemon, and sage; toss well. Cover tightly and transfer to the refrigerator to marinate for 24 hours.

2 The next day, let the chicken stand at room temperature for 30 minutes while the oven preheats to 450°F.

3 Sprinkle the chicken all over with the seasoning. Divide the lemon and sage into two piles in a roasting pan, and place the chicken, skin side up, on top.

4 Roast until the chicken is cooked through and an instant-read thermometer inserted in the thickest part of the thigh reads 165°F, about 40 minutes. For extra-crisp, golden skin, broil the chicken for the last few minutes of cooking time. Let the chicken stand for 5 minutes before carving.

NOTE If grilling, preheat a grill to medium-high heat and follow the directions for the chicken halves. Put the chicken on the grill bone side down, and grill for 30 minutes, then flip and grill until the skin is golden brown and the meat is cooked through (an instant-read thermometer inserted in the thickest part of the thigh reads 165°F), about 30 minutes more. Let the chicken stand for 5 minutes before carving.

OIL

We like to use a variety of oils in the Blue Ribbon kitchens and we encourage home cooks to do the same.

For deep-frying, when we opened the restaurant, we started out by relying on peanut oil. It gives fried food a great taste and it is tremendously stable even in extreme heat. More recently, with nut allergies becoming more of a concern, we had to look for an alternative. Eventually, after a fair amount of trial and error, we found it in soy oil. While soy doesn't impart that same rich flavor as peanut, it does have an even greater stability that makes frying a snap. You can use either one.

Canola oil is our go-to when we need a light oil for dressings or marinades or for sautéing. It's a nice, flavor-neutral, monounsaturated fat that is perfect when you don't want the strong flavor of peanut or olive oil. Canola oil will take on the flavors of other oils really well, too. Sometimes we'll make up a vinaigrette with canola, then add a drizzle of a very intense, flavorful extra-virgin olive oil.

Likewise, you can try out the various nut oils on the market. Add a few drops of walnut or hazelnut oil to a vinaigrette to give it a warm, nutty profile. This is just the thing to try with more assertive mustard vinaigrettes, where the delicate flavor of a fine extra-virgin olive oil would be lost.

When you're looking for that one-of-a-kind flavor only olive oil has, we say it's worthwhile to pay the extra money for a very fine extra-virgin. We tend to prefer oils that aren't too grassy but have a balanced yet nuanced flavor, and we lean toward Spanish olive oil with its lighter taste profile. Italian oils generally have a more intense flavor that threatens to overpower certain dishes, though we love it in small amounts.

For sautéing, when the heat would destroy a lot of the nuance of the finer extra-virgin olive oil, we use regular pure olive oil, then finish the dish with a drizzle of the good stuff to add a little flavor. Though, if we're using a low flame, as we would for fish, then we might use extra-virgin throughout for that great flavor and just to keep it simple.

There are so many variables. We say, go ahead and experiment with your favorite oils and you'll figure out what works best in your kitchen.

SEARED LONG ISLAND DUCK BREAST
WITH ORANGE-CASSIS SAUCE

SERVES 4

When our dad took us to Paris when we were little kids, we used to love to go to a restaurant right off Rue Saint-Germain called Bistro Henri. It was one of those places that epitomized French bistro cooking, which became one of the guiding influences of our restaurant. Their number-one dish was a golden, crackling-skinned, seared duck breast, served ruby rare with an intense, sweet-tart cassis sauce. The slices were arranged on the plate just so, with every sliver of fat lined up like a perfect Japanese fan, and it was the first time we had ever seen anything like that. It was also the first time we'd ever seen rare duck. It was such a pleasure to eat, so tender and glistening with a mild sweetness from the sauce. When we opened Blue Ribbon we knew rare and crispy duck breast would have to have a permanent place on the menu, and it has ever since. Garnish with orange segments, if you like.

ORANGE-CASSIS SAUCE

1½ tablespoons unsalted butter, softened

1 tablespoon all-purpose flour

2 tablespoons granulated sugar

1 tablespoon dark brown sugar

½ cup freshly squeezed orange juice

2 tablespoons red wine vinegar

1 teaspoon freshly squeezed lemon juice

2 cups chicken stock, homemade (page 247) or purchased

Perfect Sauté Seasoning (page 251) or salt and freshly ground white or black pepper

DUCK

4 Pekin duck breasts, or 2 magret duck breasts (2 to 3 pounds each)

Perfect Sauté Seasoning (page 251) or salt and freshly ground white or black pepper

1 tablespoon crème de cassis

Chopped fresh chives, for garnish

1 Preheat the oven to 400°F.

2 MEANWHILE MAKE THE SAUCE: In a small dish, combine the butter and flour until it forms a smooth paste (you can use a fork or your fingers).

3 In a large nonreactive saucepan over medium heat, combine the sugars and cook, swirling, until the mixture is melted, bubbling, and caramelized, about

recipe continues

7 minutes. Pour in the orange juice, vinegar, and lemon juice. Stir until the caramel has melted. Add the stock and bring to a simmer. Sprinkle with the seasoning. Whisk in the butter mixture and cook until slightly thickened (use caution, the butter may spatter), 1 to 2 minutes. Cover and keep warm. (Or you can make this sauce up to a day ahead and refrigerate it; reheat over low heat.)

4   TO COOK THE DUCK: Trim all the excess fat from the breasts that you can without disturbing the skin. Use a very sharp knife to score the skin in a crosshatch pattern (do not pierce the meat), then sprinkle all over with the seasoning.

5   Heat a large, heavy skillet over medium-high heat until very hot. Add the duck skin side down. Cook until the duck has released some fat and the skin has turned golden brown, 4 to 6 minutes. Pour off the excess fat from the pan (reserve it for another use; see page 35).

6   Transfer the pan to the oven and roast for 6 to 10 minutes, depending on the thickness of the meat and how you prefer it cooked (130°F on an instant-read thermometer for medium-rare). Pour the excess fat from the pan, turn the breasts over, and let rest in the pan off the heat for 5 minutes.

7   Transfer the duck to a cutting board and slice it thin against the grain. Add the crème de cassis to the pan, bring it to a simmer over low heat, and scrape up any browned bits stuck to the bottom. Pour the crème de cassis and accumulated drippings into the sauce. Drizzle the duck with the warm sauce and serve, garnished with the chives.

blue ribbon wisdom

DUCK BREAST TIPS Three types of duck breasts are commonly found on the market: magret (Moulard), Muscovy, and Pekin. Pekins and Muscovy are smaller than magrets and you will need one per person. Magrets are thicker and larger and have more external fat (which renders away). If you are using magrets, you'll need a longer cooking time than with Pekin and Muscovy. This is why we give a range in the recipe.

SHRIMP PROVENÇAL
WITH PERNOD

||||||||||||||||||||||||||||||||
SERVES 2 TO 4
||||||||||||||||||||||||||||||||

The tiny Provençal town of Venasque, which was the scene of many of our culinary and philosophical revelations, was also home to a family-run restaurant called Les Ramparts. Les Ramparts sat on the highest point of the outer wall of the fortress-like village, and it was one of the medieval enclave's only two restaurants. Politics, sports, relationships, even the arrival of a crazy band of Americans who infiltrated their town were among the topics of discussion.

But Les Ramparts had one other surprise: a great chef with one perfect dish, shrimp Provençal. We would beg to sit facing the slightly obscured kitchen, eagerly awaiting the call of *"attention au feu."* We would watch in awe as the Pernod-fueled flames danced toward the ceiling above glistening prawns still in their shells and the room filled with the sweet smell of licorice. It was intoxicating, and every order drew us deeper and deeper into the world of cooking.

½ cup Garlic Butter (page 245), cold and cut into cubes

Perfect Sauté Seasoning (page 251) or salt and freshly ground white pepper

1⅓ pounds large shrimp, peeled and deveined

1 cup Pernod

¼ cup finely sliced fresh spinach leaves

Chopped fresh flat-leaf parsley leaves, for garnish

Saffron Rice (page 138), for serving (optional)

Melt ¼ cup of the garlic butter in a large skillet over high heat. Season the shrimp, then add to the skillet and cook, tossing occasionally, for 1 minute. Pour in the Pernod and simmer until the mixture is reduced by half, about 2 minutes. Push the shrimp to one side of the pan and whisk in the remaining butter, a little at a time, until fully incorporated. Add the spinach and cook, stirring together with the shrimp, until just wilted, about 1 minute. Sprinkle with parsley and serve with saffron rice, if desired.

GRILLED SALMON
WITH MUSTARD SAUCE

SERVES 4

One mistake we will never make again is scheduling an investor party prior to actually finishing a restaurant. Autumn 1992 found Blue Ribbon still deep in construction. Since we were literally building the joint by ourselves, there wasn't anyone else to blame, so we were hesitant to call the investors and tell them that we would not be able to hold the party that we had, many months earlier, assured them would not be a problem. We put up a large curtain to cover the most unsightly areas, rented folding chairs and tables, organized a makeshift bar, and came up with a couple of quick and easy dishes. With the exception of forgetting that there was no door handle on the front door (which Eric installed just after the first guests complained about having to pull a drywall screw to get inside) and realizing that we had no mixers after the first gin and tonic was ordered, the night went off without a hitch. The salmon dish that our partner Suzanne Allgair whipped together that night was a hit, and it has been one of the most popular dishes on the menu for over fifteen years.

1½ pounds asparagus

4 (6- to 7-ounce) skinless salmon fillets, rinsed and patted dry

4 teaspoons extra-virgin olive oil

Perfect Sauté Seasoning (page 251) or salt and freshly ground white or black pepper

¼ cup Mustard Sauce (page 237)

Lemon wedges, for serving

1   Fill a large pot with 1 inch water and bring to a simmer. Put the asparagus in a steamer basket and steam, covered, until the asparagus are tender, 3 to 4 minutes.

2   Heat a grill pan over high heat until very hot. Coat the salmon fillets evenly with the oil; sprinkle both sides with the seasoning. Grill the fillets, without moving, for 5 minutes. Turn the fillets and continue to cook until the fish is just opaque and flakes easily when pierced with a fork, about 5 minutes more.

3   Top each fillet with a dollop of mustard mayonnaise. Garnish the plates with asparagus and lemon wedges and serve.

GRILLED RED TROUT
WITH STRING BEANS, BACON, AND ALMONDS

SERVES 4

Along with roast chicken, beef bourguignon, and coq au vin, trout amandine is one of those iconic dishes that we think once defined French cuisine for many Americans, at least when we were growing up. And there's good reason; trout amandine is exactly the kind of classic yet simple dish that we never get tired of. We've lightened up our version, substituting a vibrant vinaigrette instead of the usual heavy butter sauce, and seasoning it with earthy bacon, sesame oil, and rice wine vinegar so the flavors really pop. We like to use red trout here; it's a little flakier and sweeter than rainbow trout. But any kind of trout will work, the fresher the better. Just take care not to overcook the fish. If you've done it right, the trout flesh will be soft and rich next to the crunchy, salty trout skin. And if you usually leave the fish skin on the plate, at least try a bite here. We think there's no better fish skin out there than trout skin, at least when it comes to dinner.

VINAIGRETTE

2 tablespoons rice wine vinegar

¼ teaspoon salt

¼ teaspoon freshly ground black pepper

½ cup walnut oil

1 tablespoon sesame oil

STRING BEANS

6 ounces string beans, trimmed and cut in half

8 slices bacon (about 8 ounces), cooked until crisp, coarsely chopped

¼ cup sliced almonds, toasted (see Note)

SAUTÉED MUSHROOMS

8 tablespoons (1 stick) unsalted butter

4 teaspoons chopped shallots

½ pound cremini mushrooms, trimmed and quartered (about 2 cups)

¼ pound shiitake mushrooms, stems removed, caps quartered (about 2 cups)

Perfect Sauté Seasoning (page 251) or salt and freshly ground white or black pepper

TROUT

Perfect Sauté Seasoning (page 251) or salt and freshly ground white or black pepper

4 (8- to 10-ounce) whole red trout, butterflied (ask your fishmonger to do this for you)

4 teaspoons extra-virgin olive oil

Chopped fresh flat-leaf parsley leaves, for garnish

recipe continues

1   TO MAKE THE VINAIGRETTE: Whisk together the vinegar, salt, and pepper. Slowly whisk in the oils until incorporated. Set aside until ready to use.

2   TO MAKE THE STRING BEANS: Bring a pot of salted water to a boil. Have ready a large bowl of ice water. Add the beans to the boiling water; cook until crisp-tender, about 1½ minutes. Transfer the beans immediately to the ice water to stop the cooking. Drain well and cool. Toss the bacon, almonds, and beans together in a bowl.

3   TO COOK THE MUSHROOMS: Melt the butter in a large skillet over medium heat. Add the shallots and cook for 1 minute. Increase the heat to medium-high. Add the mushrooms and cook, stirring, until golden and softened, 3 to 5 minutes more. Sprinkle with the seasoning. Cover and keep warm.

4   TO COOK THE FISH: Heat a grill pan over high heat until very hot. Season each fish generously inside and out. Drizzle the fish with the oil. Grill the fish until the meat is opaque and flakes easily when pierced with a fork, 1½ to 2 minutes per side.

5   To serve, toss the bean salad with 6 tablespoons of the vinaigrette. Divide the mushrooms among 4 serving plates. Top each plate with a fish and drizzle with some of the remaining vinaigrette. Divide the bean salad on top. Sprinkle with parsley, and serve.

NOTE   To toast nuts, preheat the oven to 350°F. Spread the nuts in an even layer on a rimmed baking sheet and bake for 7 to 10 minutes, stirring once, until fragrant and lightly golden all over. Let cool completely.

ROASTED STRIPED BASS
WITH RED WINE SAUCE

Striped bass is one of the great local fishes on the East Coast. Midsummer and into early fall, it runs wild up and down the eastern seaboard from the Carolinas to Cape Cod. The meat is pearl white and the flavor sweet and meaty. A few years ago Bruce, after wading into the deep rushing waters of Nantucket Bay in the dark of night, was lucky enough to land a thirty-pounder. He packed that fish into the cooler and headed straight to the Blue Ribbon Bakery to hand it over to our partner, chef Sefton Stallard, who dazzled us with the numerous ways he prepared the majestic catch. It's a fish that can be steamed, sautéed, baked, or grilled, and Sefton tried them all that night, each dish as delicious as the next.

2 tablespoons extra-virgin olive oil, plus more for coating fish

1 red bell pepper, cored, seeded, and diced (about ¾ cup)

1 small zucchini, diced (about ½ cup)

2 celery ribs, diced (about 2 cups)

½ Spanish onion, diced (about ¾ cup)

½ teaspoon salt

½ teaspoon freshly ground white or black pepper

2 (6- to 7-ounce) wild striped bass fillets

½ cup Roasted Garlic Puree (page 235), for serving

½ cup chopped Roasted Tomatoes (page 230), for serving

1½ cups Red Wine Sauce (page 236), for serving

1   Heat the 2 tablespoons of oil in a large skillet over medium-high heat. Add the bell pepper, zucchini, celery, onion, ¼ teaspoon of the salt, and ¼ teaspoon of the pepper; cook, stirring constantly, for 7 to 10 minutes, until the vegetables are softened and light golden.

2   Heat a large skillet over high heat or light the grill. Season the fillets with the remaining salt and pepper and coat lightly with oil. Sear, skin side down, for 2 minutes. Turn and sear until the fish flakes with a fork, about 2 minutes.

3   To serve, spoon the sautéed vegetables onto 2 plates. Arrange a fillet on top of the vegetables and place a spoonful of each of the roasted garlic puree and roasted tomatoes on the side of the plate. Drizzle the red wine sauce over all.

PAELLA BASQUEZ

In the summer of 1994 we closed Blue Ribbon for the last two weeks in August and decided to take the crew to Europe for a culinary and wine tour of our old stomping grounds. We landed in Nice, rented a big Euro van, and the fourteen of us gallivanted around southern France before ending up in Spain.

One thing that has stuck with us ever since was the paellas that we sampled during the Spanish leg of our odyssey. The recipe changes from town to town and region to region but the cooking method is always the same. You start with a wood fire, a huge, shallow pan, and plenty of rice. Back in New York, wood fires and giant copper cooking vessels aren't easily achieved, so we modified the recipe. We precook the rice, then combine it with chicken, plenty of fresh seafood, saffron, and a spicy homemade sausage that gives the dish its complex flavor. The Basquez part is the bell pepper and peas. Feel free to play around with the ingredients, though. In Spain the sky is the limit, with variations of this dish including anything from the simplest seasonal vegetables to octopus, blood sausage, and snails. Whichever way you go, you'll end up in a happy place.

3 cups long-grain rice

¾ pound boneless chicken thighs

1 tablespoon extra-virgin olive oil

Perfect Roast Seasoning (page 251) or kosher salt and freshly ground black pepper

2¼ cups chicken stock, homemade (page 247) or purchased

¼ pound Spicy Chicken Sausage (page 246), cooked and sliced (see Note)

1 red bell pepper, cored, seeded, and diced (about ¾ cup)

Large pinch of saffron threads

1 pound clams, rinsed and scrubbed clean

¾ pound mussels, rinsed and scrubbed clean

½ pound medium shrimp, shelled and deveined

¾ cup frozen green peas

¼ pound squid, cleaned and thinly sliced

Chopped fresh flat-leaf parsley leaves, for garnish

recipe continues

1   Combine the rice with 4½ cups water in a large saucepan. Bring the liquid to a boil; reduce the heat, cover, and simmer until most of the liquid has evaporated, about 20 minutes. Remove from the heat and let stand for 5 minutes; fluff with a fork.

2   Meanwhile, preheat the broiler, arranging an oven rack 6 inches from the heat source.

3   Line a rimmed baking sheet with foil. Coat the chicken evenly with oil and season generously. Arrange the chicken flat on the baking sheet and cook until barely pink on the inside, 3 to 4 minutes per side (it will finish cooking in the paella).

4   In a large, deep skillet, combine the stock, chicken, sausage, bell pepper, and saffron. Bring to a boil over high heat and then reduce the heat to medium-low (the liquid should be at a strong simmer). Add the clams and cook for 1 minute. Add the rice, mussels, and shrimp. Cook, stirring, until most of the liquid has evaporated, about 10 minutes. Add the peas and squid and cook for 1 to 2 minutes more until the squid is cooked through. Discard any clams and mussels that have not opened. Sprinkle the paella with parsley and serve.

NOTE   We love the heavily seasoned homemade sausage for this dish, but you can absolutely use store-bought sausage. To get the same flavor, be sure to augment the seasoning with a generous pinch of fennel seed, cayenne, and paprika, because our sausage is spicy!

vegetables and sides

◧ french fries ◧ creamy mashed potatoes

◧ crunchy potato cakes ◧ oven-crisped potatoes

◧ crispy taters ◧ sautéed spinach ◧ collard greens with

browned butter ◧ steamed green beans with herb butter

◧ creamy turnip puree ◧ sweet frizzled leeks ◧ warm

eggplant and asparagus salad ◧ sweet potato puree ◧ broiled

wild mushrooms with tamari butter ◧ saffron rice

◧ couscous salad with lemon oil, mint, and cucumber

Our philosophy at Blue Ribbon has always been to serve every dish with a protein, a starch, a veg, and, no matter what, a crunchy little something. Sides tie the meal together, offering textures, flavors, and colors to complement the main event. In addition, we have a soft spot for the sides because they're such an American concept, that idea of having just a little bit more. Who are we to argue with that delicious abundance?

The key to making a great side dish is mixing and matching textures. You can interchange silky Creamy Mashed Potatoes (page 122) or Creamy Turnip Puree (page 131) and come out with a winning combination for your meaty pot roast or crisp fried chicken, but we would never send out a burger with anything other than our golden French Fries (page 121), and we give you tips on how to make them extra-crispy in your home kitchen. Or, you can go a little fancier and try out Crunchy Potato Cakes (page 123), which we started making as young Paris apprentices. They look very elegant but couldn't be simpler to prepare.

Color is also an important factor: you need something on your plate that's not brown or lighter brown. We share our secret for Sautéed Spinach (page 127), to preserve the fresh taste and color of the leafy green. Then there's the gorgeous shade of Saffron Rice (page 138), its golden hue every bit as alluring as its aromatic flavor. And Broiled Wild Mushrooms with Tamari Butter (page 137), a side dish with such a huge earthy taste that it will stand up to the heartiest of main meals. Okay, that one is brown, but its flavor is so outrageous, it just doesn't matter. Throughout this chapter we give pairing suggestions, but feel free to mix and match these sides. And go ahead and make two or three for those really special meals. Why not have just a little bit more?

FRENCH FRIES

SERVES 4

Eric spent time in the late 1980s at our friend Jonathan Waxman's legendary Jams restaurant, where he picked up what it takes to create the perfect french fry. Eric relays tales of Jonathan's obsession with cooking perfect food, and of his ability to look at dishes and techniques from every angle and exhaust every option until he was satisfied that the end result was the best that it could be. That's what great chefs do, and Jonathan certainly has inspired us throughout the years to follow his example.

Restaurants can live or die by the quality of their fries. When they are just right, they make a good steak great and can elevate a burger into an otherworldly realm. They can be bathed in gravy and cheese, dunked in ketchup or mayo, sprinkled with Cajun spice, or even drizzled with truffle oil. But no matter how you serve them, the perfect fries should be delicately crispy on the outside and buttery smooth within. So take your time with this recipe and don't stop until you have before you the perfect batch of fries that even Jonathan Waxman would be proud of.

Soy oil, for frying

1 pound russet potatoes, skin scrubbed clean, cut into ¼-inch batons

Perfect Sauté Seasoning (page 251) or salt and freshly ground white or black pepper

1 Heat the oil to 350°F. Blanch the potatoes in batches in the hot oil until a slight skin develops, about 2 minutes (see Note). Drain the fries on a paper-towel-lined plate.

2 Raise the oil temperature to 375°F and fry the potatoes in batches until they start to become golden, about 2 minutes. Pull the potatoes out of the oil and let stand for 1 minute. Drop the potatoes back into the oil and fry until golden brown, about another 2 minutes. Drain excess oil, toss the fries with the seasoning, and serve hot.

NOTE Take one or two of the fries out of the oil and blot them on a paper towel for a second. Then crack the fry and try to peel it. If the skin doesn't pull away, or if it just breaks, you have to keep the fries in the oil and let a little more skin develop. If the skin comes off nicely, then they're perfect; time to pull them out.

CREAMY MASHED POTATOES

SERVES 4

Few things in this world are more comforting than delicious, buttery mashed potatoes. All meals become better when mountainous white peaks of mash are part of the landscape. We leave ours a little lumpy, cook them with cream, and smash them by hand until the cream and potato become infused with each other's best attributes. If you like an even more rustic version, leave the skins on.

2 pounds white potatoes (about 4 medium potatoes), peeled and cut into equal-size chunks

Kosher salt

1 cup heavy cream

Salt

1 Preheat the oven to 375°F.

2 Put the potatoes in a pot, cover with water, and season with kosher salt. Bring to a boil and cook the potatoes until they fall apart, 10 to 15 minutes. Drain the potatoes in a colander and transfer to a rimmed baking sheet. Place the potatoes in the oven for 5 minutes to dry them and then transfer to a bowl.

3 In a small pot over medium heat, bring the cream to a boil. Pour the cream into the potatoes and mash together. Season with salt as needed.

CRUNCHY POTATO CAKES

At Le Recamier in Paris, where we both worked as young apprentices, we were rarely permitted to touch any food that was intended for the guests, at least at the beginning. Under the watchful eye of Chef Robert Chassat, we spent most of our time entrenched in the tasks of sweeping and mopping up. But as time progressed we moved closer to the grand but elusive cooktop. The first item that bridged the gap was the crunchy potato disk that accompanied the filet mignon. When an order came in, the chef would throw a steak on the grill while we dashed to the other side of the kitchen to peel a potato, julienne it on the razor-sharp mandoline, then run it back to the chef so he could fry it up in butter, pressing it until it melded to the shape of the pan.

Over the years those crunchy potatoes have worked their way onto our menu as a signature side. They're great with grilled or roasted meats, and we've served them for breakfast, lunch, and dinner. We make them to order at the restaurant (where potato-getting guy is still a job description), but they can be made up in advance. You can keep them covered in the fridge until you need them and they crisp up beautifully in a high-temperature oven.

2 pounds russet potatoes, peeled

1½ teaspoons Perfect Sauté Seasoning (page 251) or salt and freshly ground white or black pepper

8 tablespoons (1 stick) unsalted butter

1   Grate the potatoes on the large holes of a box grater. Squeeze out as much excess liquid as possible. Sprinkle with the seasoning.

2   Melt 2 tablespoons of the butter in a medium skillet over medium-high heat. Scatter one quarter of the potato mixture over the bottom of the pan. Press the potato down with a spatula to make an even layer. Cook without moving until dark golden on the bottom and the potato can be easily flipped using a spatula without falling apart, about 5 minutes. Flip the pancake and cook about 3 minutes more. Transfer to a paper-towel-lined plate to drain. Repeat three times with the remaining potatoes and butter, adjusting the heat as necessary so the potatoes don't burn. Cut into wedges and serve.

OVEN-CRISPED POTATOES

SERVES 4

These creamy-textured, golden brown potato wedges make a great accompaniment to fish and meat since they'll soak up some of the sauce or juices on the plate when you serve them. In fact, after you've boiled and cut them, you can even put the potatoes in the pan around a roast to cook them, so they absorb some of the fat—and a lot of flavor—from the meat. You can also serve them as finger food with dips.

1½ pounds white potatoes

Kosher salt

1 tablespoon extra-virgin olive oil

Perfect Sauté Seasoning (page 251) or salt and freshly ground white or black pepper

1 Preheat the oven to 450°F.

2 Put the potatoes in a pot, cover with water, and season the water with kosher salt. Bring to a boil and cook the potatoes for 5 minutes to soften slightly; drain well and pat the potatoes completely dry with paper towels. Allow the potatoes to cool to room temperature and then cut them into wedges.

3 Spread the potatoes in an even layer on a rimmed baking sheet. Drizzle with the oil, sprinkle with seasoning, and toss to coat. Roast, tossing occasionally, until crisp and golden, 30 to 40 minutes.

NOTE Make sure the potato is cold all the way through before cutting it into wedges. The potatoes get a little delicate after boiling and will break if they're not completely cooled.

BROMBERG BROS. BLUE RIBBON COOKBOOK

— 124 —

CRISPY TATERS

SERVES 4

We started making these in the restaurant as a time-saving way to get crispy potatoes. As opposed to our french fries, which are blanched in oil, these get boiled in water first to keep the insides soft and creamy when they are fried.

What's great about them is their versatility. They can become your perfect hash brown, or the base for a fish dish mixed with bacon and shrimp. They can be tossed with rosemary butter until they're creamy and rich, or served with toothpicks to dip into sour cream. They can even be mixed with crème fraîche or mayonnaise and herbs for a crispy potato salad to serve with steak, fish, or eggs Benedict (and they're great with hollandaise sauce).

1½ pounds white potatoes, peeled

Kosher salt

1½ cups vegetable or canola oil

Salt and freshly ground black pepper

1 Preheat the oven to 375°F.

2 Put the potatoes in a pot, cover with water, and season with kosher salt. Bring to a boil and cook the potatoes until very tender, about 15 minutes. Drain the potatoes in a colander and transfer to a rimmed baking sheet. Place the potatoes in the oven for 5 minutes to dry them and then remove them from the oven. Once they are cool enough to handle, cut the potatoes into cubes.

3 TO DEEP-FRY THE POTATOES: Fill a deep, wide skillet with about 3 inches of oil. Heat the oil until it is shimmering and it bubbles when sprinkled with water (it will register about 375°F on a deep-fat thermometer). Fry the potatoes, in batches if necessary, until golden brown, 7 to 10 minutes.

TO PAN-FRY THE POTATOES: Heat ½ inch oil in the skillet, fry the potatoes for 2 to 3 minutes, and then turn them to cook the other side.

4 Transfer the potatoes to a paper-towel-lined plate to drain. Sprinkle with salt and pepper to taste.

SAUTÉED SPINACH

SERVES 4

Spinach is a tricky vegetable to cook well. The quality and texture change from one season to the next, so a technique that works well in the fall may not be so successful in the spring. But here is one method that we have found to be excellent every time. The key is to get the pan nice and hot, add butter, and the moment the foam subsides and the butter turns a rich nutty brown, toss in the spinach. We like a little crispiness in our greens, so we let our spinach sit in the pan to get a little bit of char. Don't mix the spinach into the butter; just let it wilt, give the pan a quick toss, and shuttle the spinach directly onto the plate. The spinach ends up vibrantly green, a little crunchy and crisp, with the sweetness of the butter and the lift of salt. Delicious every time, we promise.

6 tablespoons unsalted butter or extra-virgin olive oil, plus more as needed

Perfect Sauté Seasoning (page 251) or salt and freshly ground white or black pepper

2 pounds spinach, cleaned and trimmed

Heat a large skillet over high heat. Add the butter and some seasoning. Working in batches and using additional butter and seasoning as needed, scatter the spinach in an even layer in the skillet. Let the spinach stand for 1 minute, until it just starts to brown, then briefly toss to finish wilting.

COLLARD GREENS
WITH BROWNED BUTTER

These are not your average stewed collard greens. Eric came up with this recipe by accident one day, when a case of collards showed up at the kitchen door instead of the spinach he had ordered.

At first, he didn't recognize them. He'd only seen soft, slow-stewed collards with ham hocks on steam tables in the South. He stood there looking at the collards while a pan of butter melting on the stove started to turn brown. Just before it burned, he threw the greens into the pan. They came out emerald green, crispy, very flavorful thanks to the nutty brown butter, and completely unlike the traditional recipe. They've been a staple ever since.

Look for dark green leaves that are firm, plump (as in not shriveled), and without any traces of yellow around the stems. And don't crowd the pan when you cook these; they'll release too much liquid and steam rather than sauté properly. If your skillet isn't large enough to give the greens plenty of room, use two pans or cook this in several batches.

4 tablespoons (½ stick) unsalted
    butter

Perfect Sauté Seasoning (page 251)
    or salt and freshly ground white
    or black pepper

2 bunches of collard greens, cleaned
    well, brown or yellow parts trimmed,
    leaves and stems cut into 2-inch
    pieces

Lemon wedges, for serving

In a very large sauté pan over high heat, melt 2 tablespoons of the butter. Add some seasoning and cook until the butter begins to brown and bubble, about 3 minutes. Add half the collards and stems, and let them sit undisturbed for 1 minute. Flip the collards and cook, stirring, for 1 minute more. Transfer the collards to a serving dish. Repeat with the remaining butter and collards. Taste for seasoning and serve with lemon wedges.

STEAMED GREEN BEANS
WITH HERB BUTTER

SERVES 4

This recipe for great-tasting beans slathered with herb butter is pure home cooking at its very best. Mom used to make something like this but we would insist that she cook the beans until they were devoid of every bit of color and texture. Then and only then would we eagerly eat all our veggies. Now we prefer to make a fresher version, blanching the beans so they still have crunch to them, then plunging them into ice water to keep them crisp and green. (You can do this ahead of time.) Before serving, they're heated up in a generous dollop of herb butter. These are a great side dish for a family-style dinner; we love them with steak, lamb, or roast chicken.

1 pound green beans, ends trimmed

2 tablespoons Herb Butter (page 244)

Perfect Sauté Seasoning (page 251) or salt and freshly ground white or black pepper

1 Bring a pot of salted water to a boil. Have ready a bowl of ice water. Add the green beans to the pot and boil for about 2 minutes, until crisp and tender. Immediately plunge the beans into the ice water, and when they have cooled, drain them well.

2 Melt the herb butter in a skillet. Toss the beans in the butter to coat. Season to taste and serve.

CREAMY TURNIP PUREE

SERVES 4

Turnips, which are so versatile, are prevalent in French cooking but are underused here in the States. They're a little like potatoes, yet earthier and more complex. We came up with this recipe because we wanted something along the lines of mashed potatoes that would be comforting, warming, and all-around yummy, yet with a little more dimension. Turnips have a bit of a bite so we add cream and potatoes to mellow this silky puree. It's a great twist—lighter than mashed potatoes yet equally delicious, with a mustardy edge that perks things up while still maintaining a comfort-food appeal. We especially love to serve this with something hearty and a little sweet, such as duck.

1 pound turnips, peeled

1 pound white potatoes, peeled

Kosher salt

½ cup heavy cream, warmed

¾ teaspoon Perfect Sauté Seasoning (page 251) or salt and freshly ground white or black pepper

1   Put the turnips and potatoes in a pot, cover with water, and season with kosher salt. Bring to a boil and cook the potatoes and turnips until very tender, 20 to 30 minutes; drain well.

2   Cut the turnips and potatoes into chunks if they are very large, and transfer to a food processor. Add the cream and seasoning. Puree the mixture until smooth. Taste, and adjust the seasoning if necessary. Serve hot.

SWEET FRIZZLED LEEKS

MAKES 4 CUPS

It's not intuitive to think that sprinkling sugar and salt on deep-fried leeks would actually improve their flavor, but these are a home run. We got the idea when we were making up our roasted chicken dish. We flash-fried leeks until they were golden brown, then sprinkled them, like our fries, with just a pinch of salt. But alongside the skin of the roasted chicken, the fried and salted leeks were almost too savory. So we began to think about the sweet aspects of the dish, and we spotted the sugar we use for our crème brûlée at the dessert station. The moment the leeks came out of the fryer, we hit them with a healthy amount of brown and white sugar that melted and caramelized to form a crispy sweet crust, giving the leeks a whole other dimension. You don't have to fry these right before serving; you can keep them on a paper towel in a low-temperature oven for an hour or so. And they're terrific at room temperature, too.

¼ cup light brown sugar, dried (see Blue Ribbon Wisdom, page 147)

¼ cup granulated sugar

3 leeks, white parts only, sliced into thin rounds (about ½ cup)

2 cups buttermilk

2 cups all-purpose flour

Soy oil, for frying

1   Combine the brown and granulated sugars in a bowl. Set aside.

2   Separate the leeks into rings with your fingers. Plunge into cold water to remove any grit and drain well. Soak the leeks in the buttermilk for 15 minutes; drain lightly and discard the buttermilk. Toss the leeks in the flour; shake off excess.

3   Heat about 3 inches of oil in a large, deep skillet to 375°F. Fry the leeks for 2 to 3 minutes, stirring slightly to fry evenly. Drain the leeks on a paper-towel-lined plate. Toss with the sugar mixture and serve.

WARM EGGPLANT AND ASPARAGUS SALAD

SERVES 2 TO 4

A lot of our dishes are inspired by the ingredients we already have on hand, especially for the wine bar, where we try to come up with fun, simple dishes and interesting combinations. This salad came about when we, along with our partner and buddy chef Sefton Stallard, discovered that a mix of tahini and Mexican honey makes an incredibly rich, complex dressing that's easy to prepare. With its Middle Eastern flavor, the dressing invites eggplant into the mix, and the asparagus adds a perfect green crunchiness.

SALAD

½ pound (about 24 thin stalks) asparagus, trimmed and halved on the diagonal

1 pound eggplant, trimmed and cut into ½-inch rounds

4 tablespoons extra-virgin olive oil

Perfect Sauté Seasoning (page 251) or salt and freshly ground white or black pepper

2 tablespoons freshly grated Parmesan cheese

1 tablespoon chopped fresh flat-leaf parsley leaves

DRESSING

2 tablespoons rice wine vinegar

1 tablespoon tahini

¾ teaspoon honey

6 tablespoons extra-virgin olive oil

Perfect Sauté Seasoning (page 251) or salt and freshly ground white or black pepper

1 TO MAKE THE SALAD: Bring salted water to a boil in a medium saucepan. Have ready a bowl of ice water. Add the asparagus and boil for 1 minute, or just until tender. Drain and immediately plunge into ice water; drain well.

2 Heat a grill pan over medium-high heat. Toss the eggplant with the oil and seasoning. Grill until the eggplant is golden and soft, 4 to 5 minutes per side. Cool and cut into ½-inch-thick strips.

3 TO MAKE THE DRESSING: Whisk together the vinegar, tahini, and honey. Slowly whisk in the oil and seasoning to taste.

4 Toss the vegetables with just enough dressing to coat lightly. Divide the salad among plates. Sprinkle with cheese and chopped parsley for serving.

SWEET POTATO PUREE

SERVES 4

We love to try to re-create classic dishes, drawing inspiration from our professional cooking experiences or from things we remember from childhood. This was our grandma Martha's favorite. She would always say: if the potatoes are good, there is no reason for any seasoning at all, they're perfect as they are. It's true; sweet potatoes are full of their own natural sugar, and they really don't need much to bring out their flavor. Cooked this way, sweet potatoes make a marvelous accompaniment that adds an extra dimension to whatever you're serving them with, with an unexpected sweetness where you might usually settle for a plain mashed potato.

2 pounds sweet potatoes, peeled and cubed

4 tablespoons (½ stick) unsalted butter

1   Put the sweet potatoes in a pot and cover with water. Bring to a boil and cook the sweet potatoes until tender, about 25 minutes; drain well. Pass through a food mill. The potatoes can be made ahead up to this point and refrigerated until ready to use.

2   In a large skillet, melt the butter over medium heat. Add the potato puree and stir until combined and heated through.

BROILED WILD MUSHROOMS
WITH TAMARI BUTTER

During our citywide search for perfect sushi in the summer of 1994, we stumbled past a little sushi bar not far from our apartment. We were already full from sake and an endless assortment of rolls from some of New York's top sushi places when we found ourselves settling into a drab sushi bar with brash lighting. The tiny man who stood behind the bar was barely visible from the street but his confident and welcoming smile were what had drawn us in. His chef's coat was immaculate; his knives were laid out on his cutting board as if he were about to perform surgery. And then dish after dish, slice of fish after slice of fish arrived and we fell under the master chef's spell. The rice was sweet and vinegary, the fish vibrant and fresh; and each and every knife stroke brought out more and more flavor in every bite. That night was special in so many ways, but most of all because we had found our brilliant partner, friend, and culinary cohort, Toshi Ueki, who is the chef behind all the Blue Ribbon Sushi restaurants.

One of the dishes Toshi served us that first night was this unlikely combination of sweet butter, sake, soy sauce, and earthy mushrooms, simply broiled to a gorgeous deep brown. It was one of the first major revelations we had when we were creating dishes for Blue Ribbon Sushi, and it has been on the menu since day one.

1 pound assorted wild mushrooms, such as chicken-of-the-woods, maitake, king, hedgehog, shiitake, and cremini, cleaned with a damp towel	2 tablespoons tamari or soy sauce 2 tablespoons sake 4 tablespoons (½ stick) unsalted butter

1 Preheat the broiler.

2 In a bowl, toss the mushrooms with the tamari and sake. Arrange the mushrooms on a rimmed baking sheet and dot with the butter. Broil, turning once, until tender and golden, about 5 minutes total.

SAFFRON RICE

Alonso Almeida (see page 140), who was the Blue Ribbon oyster shucker for our first twelve years, provided the inspiration for this dish. He was a busy guy and usually didn't get to come down to the kitchen with the rest of us for our regular staff meal, so every night at around 2:30 A.M. we'd ask him what he wanted to eat. He always wanted us to make him yellow rice with either chicken or shrimp. So we did—using the saffron we had around for our menu staple Paella Basquez (page 113). After years of making the recipe for Alonso, we put it on the menu as a side for our Shrimp Provençal with Pernod (page 107). It's justly popular.

½ onion, finely chopped	2 cups long-grain rice
2 tablespoons unsalted butter	1 teaspoon kosher salt
1 teaspoon saffron threads	

1 In a small saucepan, combine the onion, butter, and saffron over medium heat. Sweat the onion until it is translucent, about 3 minutes. Add the rice and stir to coat with the butter; cook for 1 minute.

2 Stir in 3½ cups water and the salt. Bring the liquid to a boil. Reduce the heat to low, cover the pan, and simmer until the liquid has almost completely evaporated, about 20 minutes. Remove from the heat and let stand, covered, for 5 minutes. Fluff with a fork.

blue ribbon wisdom

SAFFRON When buying saffron, make sure you get it from a place that sells a lot of it. You don't want to end up with a dusty old jar that's been sitting on the shelf for years. Saffron will dry out with age, and when it does it loses a little bit of its fragrance and power. You'll still be able to use it; you'll just have to use more of it to get the same effect. There are so many fantastic dishes that benefit from a pinch of saffron, from soups to fish dishes to rice and vegetables, that you should use your saffron when you buy it; don't let it sit around the pantry and get old.

Another tip for using saffron is to infuse it into a liquid before adding it to your dish. Simmer it with chicken stock, broth, milk, or water for a few minutes to bring out the tremendous flavor, then add it to whatever you are cooking. That way you won't get spots of yellow rice here and there. If you're making a soup or stew, you could also add the saffron to the onions and olive oil in the beginning when you are sautéing to give it a little bit of a toasted flavor. You do have to be a little more careful, though. Overcooking will mask the saffron's delicate flavor. Make sure to use medium, not high, heat.

COUSCOUS SALAD
WITH LEMON OIL, MINT, AND CUCUMBER

SERVES 4 TO 6

During our first visit to Israel, we became infatuated with couscous. It can take on so many forms, including a main course with meat and vegetables in a rich, spicy broth and this incarnation, a summer salad with the light fresh flavors of olive oil, lemon juice, and herbs. Plenty of parsley and mint give this vibrant dish a wonderful freshness. Serve it on its own or with grilled fish or vegetables.

4 cups cooked couscous, prepared according to package directions

1 cucumber, peeled and finely chopped

2 tomatoes, chopped

½ cup chopped fresh flat-leaf parsley leaves

¼ cup chopped fresh mint leaves

3 tablespoons extra-virgin olive oil

1½ tablespoons freshly squeezed lemon juice

1 teaspoon Perfect Sauté Seasoning (page 251) or salt and freshly ground white or black pepper

Combine the couscous, cucumber, tomatoes, parsley, mint, oil, lemon juice, and seasoning in a large bowl; toss well. Taste and adjust seasoning, if necessary.

ALONSO

From November 1992, until late 2006, there was one constant at Blue Ribbon: Alonso Almeida, the king of oyster shuckers.

On a sunny summer day in 1996, hundreds, perhaps thousands, of anxious New Yorkers clambered their way onto West Fourth Street between Broadway and Lafayette to join in New York City's first oyster festival. Up until that time oysters had fallen far from grace in the big city, a far cry from the turn of the twentieth century when penny oysters from the local beds had been listed on nearly every restaurant menu and oyster carts crowding the cobblestone streets had nourished blue-collar and white-collar workers alike. But on this day nearly four years into the young life of Blue Ribbon, the city's oyster revival was under way and the energy was high. The street was filled with music and the buzz of the excited hordes drinking beer and slurping down oysters in every combination and every dish imaginable. The scene was set for the momentous oyster-shucking contest, the real reason we were all there.

We arrived just a bit late; our competitors were already gathered on the makeshift stage. The crowd was screaming, but all knew that the show couldn't start without the man from Blue Ribbon, Alonso. We herded Alonso through the crowd like a champion boxer on his way to the ring to take on a younger opponent. The crowd parted, and outstretched hands reached to give their beloved hero a pat on the back as they yelled and chanted his name.

Alonso was like no other. When we met him in the summer of 1986 at the American Hotel in Sag Harbor where Eric was the chef, his dark hair was already speckled by the silver strands that would eventually act as a backdrop to his most distinctive feature, the Alonso headband. Back then Alonso, whose smile was as wide as it was infectious, was working as a clam shucker at Montauk's legendary Gosman's Wharf. After work, he would swing by the hotel to help his wife clean the rooms so that she could finish early and they could both get home to take care of their baby daughter. One afternoon while walking through the kitchen, Alonso discreetly handed Eric a piece of paper with something scribbled on it. He told Eric that it was a good recipe for a sauce that goes great with clams, his own creation!

Anyway, when the oyster competition began, most of the competitors launched into a shucking frenzy—shells cracked, knives searched for the perfect spot, and ice flew in every direction. But Alonso slowly and calmly adjusted his headband just so, laid out the ice on his tray to make the perfect resting spot for his beloved bivalves, pulled a glove onto his hand, and began his search for his first victim, a venerable bluepoint. By this time the others were far into their quest to be the first to shuck thirty-six oysters. Alonso was just getting rolling. We will never ever forget the immense feeling of pride that came over us. Alonso was going to lose and lose badly. He understood the competition, but that was of no interest to him. Shucking perfect oysters was all that mattered; merely getting them open had no value.

This dedication to doing things right was embodied in everything Alonso undertook. It was why when Daniel Boulud, Mario Batali, Jean-Georges Vongerichten, and the rest of New York City's great chefs would walk through the door at Blue Ribbon, they would insist on sitting in front of Alonso. It's why, year after year, customers from all over the world would bring him gifts (mainly headbands bearing his name) and send him pictures from their travels, and tell him that they couldn't wait to get back to sample his meticulous craft.

As the competition drew to a close, the attention began to drift from the men who were battling it out for speed to the beautiful platter that Alonso was creating. By the time the others were finished and the champ had been crowned, all eyes were solely on Alonso. It was an amazing moment. The place was going crazy and everyone was chanting Alonso . . . Alonso . . . Alonso! No one cared who had finished first. Once Alonso finished arranging his lemons and parsley, the bidding for the platter began. It went for about a hundred bucks and Alonso just sat back and smiled (the other sloppy platters went into the garbage). He was not the fastest by a long shot but he knew for certain that he was the best. It was never clearer to us than at that moment what Blue Ribbon stood for, and what Alonso meant to us.

Alonso's clam sauce of celery, onion, tomato, cilantro, lemon juice, and just the right amount of black pepper is still among the best things we've ever eaten. And the area at the end of the bar at Blue Ribbon where he would hold court on a nightly basis is and always will be Alonso's raw bar.

From the bottom of all our hearts, Alonso was all we strive to be.

desserts

◉ crème brûlée ◉ chocolate bruno ◉ banana walnut bread pudding with butterscotch-banana sauce ◉ baba au rhum with rum syrup ◉ baklava ◉ profiteroles with ice cream and hot fudge ◉ fresh strawberry sundae ◉ toast with strawberries, hot fudge, and honey ◉ suzanne's crisp and buttery oatmeal cookies ◉ thin and crisp chocolate chip cookies ◉ hot fudge ◉ hot fudge with honey ◉ white chocolate butterscotch with bananas

W e're sure we're not alone in having a certain love affair with the desserts we grew up on—the ones Mom used as rewards for good behavior or, more commonly, as a bribe to get us to eat our vegetables. And, for the record, we have never seen anything wrong with this kind of parenting—in fact, we applaud it! If nothing else, it makes a good excuse for us parents to try out a new dessert recipe every night.

We picked up some fantastic dessert recipes from our time in France and were happy to bring them to the States with a few adjustments. We happen to like the custard in our Crème Brûlée (page 146), which is just a little bit creamier than the average Parisian version. For our take on a dark chocolate mousse, we even imported our mentor, Chef Bruno Hess, to teach us how to make it using the ingredients available here in America. The result is Chocolate Bruno (page 149), and it has become Blue Ribbon's signature dessert.

We do love to play around with ingredients in our kitchen, and we don't limit our experiments to the savory dishes. Banana Walnut Bread Pudding with Butterscotch-Banana Sauce (page 151) and its variations are the scrumptious results of a recipe gamble that really paid off. And thanks go to our partner and friend Suzanne Allgair, who tinkered with the Baklava (page 156) to get a uniquely mouthwatering version of the traditional Middle Eastern pastry.

We're not shy about including those childhood favorites, either. A Fresh Strawberry Sundae (page 160) might not be the most sophisticated close to a meal, but we're hard-pressed to name one that's more universally beloved. That's why we serve classics like this at our restaurant and think they have a rightful place in our homes, too.

CRÈME BRÛLÉE

This classic custard is one of those desserts that everyone wants to know how to perfect. We like ours a little less sweet than usual, and we use deep custard dishes instead of the more standard shallow gratin dishes, so that you can really dig your spoon in. Shattering the brittle sugar crust adds an element of excitement and textural contrast to the silky smooth, vanilla-flecked custard underneath. And our version manages to be extraordinarily creamy, rich, and light all at once.

1 vanilla bean

11 large egg yolks

1 cup granulated sugar

1 quart heavy cream

¼ cup light brown sugar, dried (see Note)

1 Preheat the oven to 300°F.

2 Using a small, sharp knife, split the vanilla bean in half lengthwise and scrape the seeds into a bowl; reserve the pod. Add the egg yolks and ¾ cup of the granulated sugar and whisk until thick and yellow (whisk the mixture immediately to prevent the sugar from "cooking" the eggs).

3 In a medium pot, combine the cream and reserved vanilla bean pod. Bring the cream to a boil over medium-high heat. Immediately remove from the heat; discard the pod. Whisking constantly, pour a small amount of the cream into the egg yolk mixture. Add the rest, a little at a time, until the cream is fully incorporated. Strain through a fine-mesh sieve.

4 Pour the custard into ten (4-ounce) ramekins. Skim off any air bubbles from the surface of the custards. Transfer the ramekins to an ovenproof baking dish. Transfer the baking dish to the oven and pour hot water into the baking dish to come halfway up the sides of the ramekins. Bake until the custard is firm but not brown, 35 to 45 minutes. If you tap the ramekin, the center wiggle should be a ring about the size of a nickel. (Do not overcook or the eggs will curdle.) Remove the ramekins from the baking dish and let cool slightly at room temperature; transfer to the refrigerator to cool completely. The custard can be made up to 3 days ahead.

5 To make the brittle tops of the custards, preheat the broiler, with an oven rack at least 4 inches from the heat source.

6 Combine the brown sugar and the remaining ¼ cup granulated sugar in a bowl. Arrange the ramekins on a rimmed baking sheet. Sprinkle the top of each custard evenly with a thin layer of the sugar mixture. Transfer the baking sheet to the oven and broil until the sugar melts and turns golden, 1 to 1½ minutes (watch carefully to see that it does not burn). Let stand 1 minute before serving.

blue ribbon wisdom

DRYING BROWN SUGAR Drying brown sugar before using it for crème brûlée topping helps eliminate any lumps, giving you the smoothest possible caramelized crust. To dry brown sugar, spread it on a rimmed baking sheet and toast in a 250°F oven until dry to the touch, about 20 minutes. Let cool completely, then press through a sieve.

ON TRULY CREAMY CRÈME What makes this crème brûlée special is its thick custard and the smooth texture you feel in every bite. Make sure to whip the egg yolks sufficiently to fully incorporate the sugar. Otherwise this dish has a tendency to separate and will never really set up. The mixture should be pale yellow and thicken to a ribbon-like consistency.

CHOCOLATE BRUNO

SERVES 6

October 25, 1992. One week prior to opening Blue Ribbon, we place a call to Paris: "Bruno, help!"

The faint reply from the other side of the ocean: "Don't worry, guys, I'll be there. Besides, I could use a break."

And with that, our mentor, Chef Bruno Hess from Le Recamier restaurant in Paris, was on his way to the rescue.

Bruno worked four nearly twenty-four-hour days in a row, sleeping on the floor of the dining room while helping us get to opening day. Some break!

One of the nights during his stay we attacked the famed Fondant Chocolat, a dense chocolate mousse that was one of Bruno's specialties in Paris. Due to the differences between American and French eggs and butter, we couldn't get the recipe to work at all. We were incredibly frustrated; it was something we'd made hundreds of times before in France, so why wasn't it coming out right in SoHo? By sunrise, and several hundreds of eggs later, we arrived at something completely different but perhaps even more delicious than the original. It could no longer be called Fondant Chocolat. Voilà, the birth of Chocolate Bruno.

5 ounces white chocolate, chopped

2 ounces graham crackers (½ sleeve, or 4 full crackers), crushed (1 cup)

18 ounces semisweet chocolate, chopped

1 cup (2 sticks) plus 3 tablespoons unsalted butter

3 tablespoons brewed espresso

8 large egg yolks

8 large egg whites

1 tablespoon sugar

Unsweetened cocoa powder, for serving

Hot Fudge (page 166), for serving

Raspberries, for serving (optional)

Line the bottom of 6 (8-ounce) ramekins with parchment or wax paper. In the top of a double boiler or in a bowl set over (but not touching) a pan of simmering water, melt the white chocolate; stir in the graham crackers. Divide equally among the prepared molds, using a spoon to spread evenly on each base. Refrigerate until firm, about 2 hours.

recipe continues

2   In the top of a double boiler or in a bowl set over (but not touching) a pan of simmering water, melt the semisweet chocolate and butter with the espresso. Let cool for 2 minutes. Stir in (do not whisk) the yolks until just incorporated.

3   In the bowl of an electric mixer fitted with the whisk attachment, beat the whites until foamy. Slowly add the sugar and increase the speed. Beat until the whites form soft, floppy peaks.

4   Fold a little bit of the whites into the chocolate mixture to lighten it, then gently fold in the remaining egg whites. Spoon the mousse into the molds and level the tops with an offset spatula or spoon. Chill until set, about 3 hours or overnight.

5   To serve, gently dip the bottoms of the ramekins in a bowl of hot water for 30 seconds to 1 minute. Run a spatula along the edges of each ramekin (outside the parchment paper) and pop out the mousse. Remove the paper. Transfer the desserts to plates and dust with cocoa powder. Serve with a drizzle of hot fudge and raspberries, if desired.

NOTE Pregnant women, the elderly, and people who have compromised immune systems should exercise caution when consuming the raw eggs in this recipe.

blue ribbon wisdom

CHOCOLATE, WHITE AND OTHERWISE White chocolate can be a pretty sketchy product if you don't know what you're looking for. Read the ingredients and check for cocoa butter, which is the only thing about white chocolate that's related to chocolate at all! If it's not made with real cocoa butter, chances are the manufacturer is substituting cheap hydrogenated vegetable oils instead—resulting in a product euphemistically called "white confectionary tablet."

You might be surprised that this recipe calls for semisweet rather than bittersweet chocolate. There's a reason, of course. Calling for semisweet chocolate allows us to use less sugar when beating the eggs whites, which makes a looser, lighter meringue. This keeps the Bruno mousse-like and fluffy rather than dense.

BANANA WALNUT BREAD PUDDING
WITH BUTTERSCOTCH-BANANA SAUCE

During one of the early days after we first opened the Blue Ribbon Market, we got it in our heads to fill the display shelves with a variety of our gorgeous homemade breads. We soon realized that we had grossly underestimated our shelf space. We had to make hundreds of loaves to make it look full—way more than we could sell.

As if on cue, a French chef (who shall remain nameless) walked into the crazy Bromberg brothers' bread extravaganza and said he wanted to buy some loaves of white bread to make bread pudding. We were surrounded by baguettes and feeling somewhat frustrated. "You're welcome to take any bread you want," we told him. And he looked at us, horrified, saying, "No, no, I need *pain de mie*!" He walked out, disgusted that we didn't have the proper pullman white bread for bread pudding.

As soon as he left we decided to prove him wrong. We started cutting up all those baguettes and folded the pieces into the custard we had made for crème brûlée. Then we played around and added different flavorings to different batches (banana walnut turned out to be our favorite), and cooked it all in a water bath. While baking, our puddings smelled sweet, yeasty, and eggy, and they came out golden brown, crunchy on the outside and custardy smooth on the inside. We haven't used a traditional bread pudding recipe since.

1 vanilla bean

11 large egg yolks

1 cup sugar

1 quart heavy cream

1 (12-ounce) baguette or other white bread, cut into 1-inch cubes (about 10 cups)

1 pound bananas, peeled and sliced ½-inch thick (2 to 4 bananas)

¾ cup chopped walnuts, toasted (see Note, page 111)

Butterscotch-Banana Sauce (page 167)

| Using a small, sharp knife, split the vanilla bean in half lengthwise and scrape the seeds into a bowl; reserve the pod. Add the egg yolks and ¾ cup of the sugar and whisk until thick and yellow (whisk the mixture immediately to prevent the sugar from "cooking" the eggs).

recipe continues

2 In a medium pot, combine the cream, the remaining ¼ cup sugar, and the reserved vanilla bean pod. Bring the cream to a boil over medium-high heat, stirring to dissolve the sugar. Immediately remove from the heat; discard the pod. Whisking constantly, pour a small amount of the cream into the egg yolk mixture. Add the rest, a little at a time, until the cream is fully incorporated. Strain through a fine-mesh sieve. You can make the custard up to 1 day ahead and store it, covered, in the refrigerator.

3 Grease a 9 × 13-inch baking pan. Combine the bread, bananas, and walnuts in the pan, making sure everything is well distributed. Pour in just enough custard mixture to completely cover the bread (you may have some leftover; save it). Let stand for at least 20 minutes and up to an hour (or let it rest overnight in the refrigerator). If the bread absorbs all the custard, top it off with a little more. Then firmly press the bread down into the custard so it's submerged.

4 Preheat the oven to 350°F.

5 Cover the pan with foil. Place the pudding pan in a larger pan, adding just enough hot water to the larger pan to come halfway up the sides of the pudding pan. Bake until the pudding is lightly set and a knife inserted in the center comes out almost clean, 1 to 1½ hours. The pudding may be kept, covered, in the refrigerator for up to 3 days and reheated to serve. Before serving, drizzle with the Butterscotch-Banana Sauce.

blue ribbon wisdom

VARIATIONS Bread pudding can take on a lot of forms. If you love fruit, you can make it with fruit; if you love chocolate, you can make it with chocolate; if you love walnuts and candied ginger . . . The banana and chocolate versions are the most popular, so we always have them on the menu. But we still like to come up with new flavors, and they've all been well received—especially rum raisin, apple and dried cherry, and even a version with lychee, which is a great complement to the menu at Blue Ribbon Sushi. So let your taste buds be your guide, and come up with your own house favorite.

BABA AU RHUM
WITH RUM SYRUP

The inspiration for this dessert dates back to our days as apprentices in Paris. We were working at Bistro de Louvre under the direction of Chef Bruno Hess (of Chocolate Bruno fame; see page 149), getting a great education just from sneaking tastes of everything that came out of the kitchen. But there was one dish that the waiters served up from the bar: *baba au rhum*. Kept in a large glass vessel, the delicate little cakes floated in a golden syrup, and throughout the evening the chef and pastry chef would constantly poke and prod the contents of this mysterious jar. We developed a forbidden fruit–style obsession with it.

When we finally got the chance to taste the baba, we decided it was one of the best things ever. The cake was spongy and seemed able to absorb a seemingly endless amount of syrup without ever falling apart. Sprinkled with berries or even just a touch of confectioners' sugar, it was a stylish and grown-up dessert, and with the amount of rum that was in it, you could see why it was served up from the bar. We put this quintessential rum dessert on the menu the moment we opened our wine bar. In the beginning we probably ate more than we sold, but now it's definitely one of our most popular items.

BABA CAKES

¼ cup whole milk, lukewarm (see Blue Ribbon Wisdom)

¼ ounce fresh yeast or 1 teaspoon active dry yeast

2 large eggs

1 cup all-purpose flour

3 tablespoons sugar

1 ½ teaspoons honey

Pinch of salt

10 tablespoons (1¼ sticks) unsalted butter, cubed, at room temperature

RUM SYRUP

¾ cup sugar

½ cup dark rum

Whipped cream, for serving

Fresh fruit, for serving

1   TO MAKE THE CAKES: Lightly grease or spray with nonstick cooking spray each cup of a 12-cup muffin pan. In the bowl of an electric mixer fitted with the paddle

attachment, combine the milk and the yeast. Let rest, allowing the yeast to ferment, for 1 hour.

2   Add the eggs and mix until combined. Add the flour, sugar, honey, and salt and mix until a stiff batter forms. With the mixer running, add the butter, one cube at a time, and continue mixing until the butter is completely incorporated.

3   Pour the batter into the prepared muffin cups; each cup should be a little more than halfway full. Cover with plastic wrap and let rise in a warm spot for 1 hour.

4   Preheat the oven to 375°F.

5   Bake the babas for 20 to 25 minutes, or until fully puffed and pulling away from the sides of the cups and a uniform golden brown color. Allow them to cool slightly in the pan, about 5 minutes, then turn out onto a wire rack to finish cooling. Store in an airtight container at room temperature for up to 3 days.

6   TO MAKE THE SYRUP: Pour the sugar, ½ cup water, and the rum into a saucepan over medium-high heat and bring to a boil. Reduce the heat to medium and let simmer until the sugar has completely dissolved, 3 to 5 minutes. Let cool and refrigerate, covered, until needed or for up to 2 weeks.

7   Just before serving, pour the rum syrup over the cakes. Top with a dollop of whipped cream and the fresh fruit of your choice.

blue ribbon wisdom

WORKING WITH YEAST   Anytime you work with yeast, the temperature of the ingredients needs to be closely monitored. The milk should really be tepid when you mix it in. If it's too cold, the mixture will take forever to rise; too warm and you'll kill the yeast and the whole thing is over before it even starts. And don't skimp on the mixing time or rising time. Follow all the steps and the reward will be light and airy baked goods.

BAKLAVA

MAKES ABOUT 20 PIECES

In Paris, Suzanne Allgair, our childhood friend and now business partner, used to frequent an obscure, immaculate little street on the Left Bank lined with Turkish food stands. In the glass cases, filled with exotic pastries and manned by effusive vendors vying for the customers' attention, the baklava would glow like gold in the sun, and we developed an infatuation for this crunchy, nutty, obscenely sweet and sticky Middle Eastern confection. For the Blue Ribbon Market, Suzanne was determined to perfect her version, since a lot of baklava is a little too dense and a lot too sweet. Using kataifi, which is finely shredded phyllo dough, makes the pastry much lighter and less sugary. The kataifi stays crunchy and crispy and breaks up easily, making it very, very easy to eat in embarrassingly large amounts.

HONEY SYRUP	BAKLAVA
1 cup honey	½ pound kataifi (see Note), defrosted
½ cup sugar	2 cups chopped walnuts
¾ teaspoon grated orange zest	¼ cup sugar
¾ teaspoon grated lemon zest	½ teaspoon ground cinnamon
½ cinnamon stick	¼ teaspoon ground cloves
	1 cup (2 sticks) unsalted butter, melted

1 TO MAKE THE HONEY SYRUP: In a medium saucepan over high heat, stir together the honey, sugar, orange zest, lemon zest, and cinnamon stick with ½ cup water and bring to a boil. Reduce the heat to medium and simmer, uncovered, for 10 minutes. The syrup can be made in advance and stored in an airtight container at room temperature.

2 TO MAKE THE BAKLAVA: Preheat the oven to 350°F. Divide the kataifi into 5 even piles.

3 In a food processor, combine the walnuts, sugar, cinnamon, and cloves. Process to a sandy consistency.

4 Detangle the first pile of kataifi and spread evenly over the bottom of an 8 × 8-inch baking pan. Sprinkle one fourth of the walnut mixture evenly over the kataifi. Repeat, alternating the kataifi and nuts until all ingredients are used; end with a kataifi layer.

5 When the pan is evenly layered, use a long sharp knife to cut the pastry into 2-inch triangles, making sure the dough is cut all the way through to the bottom of the pan. Spoon the melted butter over the pastry.

6 Transfer the pan to the oven and bake until the top is crispy and golden brown, 35 to 45 minutes. Let stand for 10 minutes and then spoon the honey syrup over the pastry. Cover and let rest in the pan at room temperature for at least 6 hours and up to overnight before serving.

NOTE Kataifi can be found in larger supermarkets or smaller boutique markets, but if it's unavailable in your area you can substitute 1 pound of phyllo dough. Defrost and julienne the phyllo, then carry on with the recipe. The julienned phyllo will soak up the syrup faster than the kataifi and will need to rest for only 1 or 2 hours before serving.

PROFITEROLES
WITH ICE CREAM AND HOT FUDGE

SERVES 4

Profiteroles are something we used to have often at Le Recamier, in Paris, where we both worked after cooking school. Over there we'd stuff the puffs with pastry cream and drizzle a bitter chocolate sauce around them. When we were coming up with our dessert menu, we wanted something more decadent and, well, fun. We decided to fill them with ice cream and top them with our hot fudge sauce.

1 cup whole milk

4 tablespoons (½ stick) unsalted
   butter

½ cup all-purpose flour

4 large eggs

Vanilla, chocolate, and strawberry
   ice cream

Hot Fudge (page 166), for serving

1 In a saucepan over medium heat, simmer the milk and butter until the butter is completely melted. Remove from the heat and quickly stir in the flour with a wooden spoon. Place the pan back onto the heat and stir until the mixture gets quite dry, 3 to 5 minutes. The mixture should come together in a large ball.

2 Transfer the mixture to the bowl of an electric mixer. Add 3 of the eggs, one at a time, and beat well after each addition. Cover the dough with plastic wrap and refrigerate for at least 2 hours and up to 2 days.

3 Preheat the oven to 450°F. Line a baking sheet with parchment paper.

4 Transfer the dough to a pastry bag fitted with a medium round tip. Fill the pastry bag with the dough. Pipe out 2-tablespoon drops of dough onto the prepared sheet, making sure to stagger the drops for even baking.

5 Whisk the remaining egg. Using the back of a spoon, brush the egg onto each drop, smoothing the tops. Bake for 25 to 30 minutes until puffed and golden brown. Remove from the oven. When cool enough to handle, use a knife to make a slit in the side of each profiterole to let out steam.

6 Serve 3 profiteroles to a plate. Cut each in half and fill with ice cream, put on the tops, and cover with hot fudge.

FRESH STRAWBERRY SUNDAE

Why serve a strawberry sundae? Because it's pretty! And incredibly satisfying. Seriously, when strawberries are in season and you pair them with a good-quality ice cream, this picture-perfect pink sundae is a gorgeous tribute to the fruit.

Part of our vision at Blue Ribbon is serving idealized versions of what you'd get at a diner, and our homemade hot fudge is the key to making really special sundaes. Growing up, we'd scoop our ice cream into bowls, then wait impatiently as the bottle of Bosco or Hershey's syrup bubbled gently in the copper double boiler on Mom's stove. Now we top our ice cream with a silky smooth, ultra-rich combination of cream and chocolate.

Hot Fudge (page 166)   Whipped cream, for serving

4 scoops (½ pint) strawberry ice cream   Sliced strawberries, for serving

Swirl a dollop of hot fudge into the bottom of a chilled sundae glass. Add a scoop of strawberry ice cream, add more hot fudge, then another scoop of ice cream. Top with more hot fudge, whipped cream, and sliced strawberries. Repeat for the second sundae.

VARIATION ▢ HOMEMADE HOT FUDGE SUNDAE

Substitute vanilla ice cream for strawberry ice cream and toasted chopped walnuts for the strawberries.

TOAST
WITH STRAWBERRIES, HOT FUDGE, AND HONEY

SERVES 6

In those early weeks of Blue Ribbon Bakery Market, before the toast craze really caught on, we had a fair amount of time every day to chat with Andy Morgan, our manager. After the shelves were filled with fresh baked breads and the cold cases overflowed with smoked fish, meats, and cheeses, we would talk about music, ladies, life, our quandaries and wonders, our travels, politics, sports, and yes, what amazing toasts we could come up with that would entice the passersby to come into our new store. Andy was one of a kind. He was exuberant and thrilled with life. When he spoke of his pilgrimage to Nepal or his spur-of-the-moment cycle from Seattle to Dallas, his pale freckled complexion would turn a soft shade of red to match his rusty-colored hair. His smile would widen and widen until you thought that it was going to burst and he would shyly offer up a profound statement that made everything feel just right. Andy saw things in a simple light; he loved life and all that it had to offer and, as it turned out, he also loved sweets.

But it wasn't until one fateful day when one of our patrons was dismayed to hear that we had nothing sweet that our redheaded cohort made the leap from the world of toasts dominated by savory combinations of vegetables, meats, dips, spreads, and cheeses to one of chocolate, berries, and luscious honey. Andy came up with this sweet toast that is perfect for a morning snack, an afternoon nibble, or a late-night dessert. Strawberry shortcake, eat your heart out!

We miss Andy and his sweet memory lives with us every day.

6 tablespoons good-quality honey, preferably Mexican (see sidebar, page 29)

6 (1-inch) slices challah, homemade (page 200) or your favorite store-bought soft loaf, lightly toasted

1 pint strawberries, hulled and sliced

6 tablespoons Hot Fudge, homemade (page 166) or purchased

Confectioners' sugar, for sprinkling

Slather the honey over the toast slices. Divide the berries evenly among the toasts. Top each slice with a drizzle of hot fudge, and then sprinkle with confectioners' sugar. Serve immediately.

SUZANNE'S CRISP AND BUTTERY
OATMEAL COOKIES

MAKES 24 COOKIES

Our partner Suzanne Allgair, our guru of everything sweet, pulled this recipe out of her mother Janet's repertoire. We tweaked the recipe just a bit to make it a little crisper and a little more buttery, which we think enhances the oatmeal cookie experience. The balance of earthy oats and subtle sweetness has made it a big hit with cookie fans of all kinds.

1 cup (2 sticks) unsalted butter, at room temperature

1 cup granulated sugar

½ cup (packed) dark brown sugar

1 large egg, at room temperature

1 teaspoon vanilla extract

1½ cups all-purpose flour

1 teaspoon ground cinnamon

1 teaspoon baking soda

Pinch of salt

1½ cups old-fashioned oats

1 cup golden raisins

1 cup chopped pecans, lightly toasted (see Note, page 111)

1 Preheat the oven to 350°F. Line 2 baking sheets with parchment paper.

2 In the bowl of an electric mixer, cream together the butter and the sugars until light and fluffy, 2 to 4 minutes. Scrape down the sides of the bowl and add the egg and vanilla; beat to combine.

3 In a small bowl, mix the flour, cinnamon, baking soda, and salt. Add the dry ingredients to the mixer in three additions, scraping down the sides of the bowl between each addition. Mix until just combined and then stir in the oats, raisins, and pecans.

4 Roll the dough into 1-inch balls and place on the baking sheets. Leave at least 2 inches of space around each cookie. Bake for 15 to 18 minutes, until the cookies are golden brown and just set (they will crisp up as they cool). Transfer the cookies to a wire rack to cool.

THIN AND CRISP CHOCOLATE CHIP COOKIES

MAKES 24 COOKIES

Seeing that over half of the cookies consumed in this country are of the chocolate chip variety, there are many different visions of the perfect form. Some people like them soft and chewy; some people like them crisp and dunkable. We've noticed that people generally like the version that they grew up on. Since our inspiration for cookies stems from our mom serving them up after school with a cold glass of milk, we land firmly in camp crispy. These are delightfully thin and delicate. The caramel flavor of the brown sugar underscored with just the right balance of salt always makes us happy.

1 cup (2 sticks) unsalted butter, at room temperature

1 cup (packed) dark brown sugar

½ cup granulated sugar

1 large egg, at room temperature

1 tablespoon vanilla extract

2 cups all-purpose flour

1 teaspoon baking soda

½ teaspoon salt

2 cups semisweet chocolate chips

1   Preheat the oven to 350°F. Line 2 baking sheets with parchment paper.

2   In the bowl of an electric mixer, cream together the butter and the sugars until light and fluffy, 2 to 4 minutes. Scrape down the sides of the bowl and add the egg and vanilla; beat to combine.

3   In a small bowl, mix the flour, baking soda, and salt. Add the dry ingredients to the mixer in three additions, scraping down the sides of the bowl between each addition. Mix until just combined and then stir in the chocolate chips.

4   Roll the dough into 1-inch balls and place on the baking sheets. Leave at least 2 inches of space around each cookie. Bake for 15 to 18 minutes, until the cookies are golden brown and just set (they will crisp up as they cool). Transfer the cookies to a wire rack to cool.

HOT FUDGE

MAKES 2 CUPS

This is our traditional hot fudge, made with just the right balance of chocolate and corn syrup. It's a user-friendly recipe that never separates, and it gets perfectly sticky on top of ice cream. You can make a batch and use it right away, or refrigerate it or even freeze it.

12 ounces semisweet chocolate, chopped

1 cup heavy cream

¼ cup light corn syrup

Combine the chocolate, cream, and corn syrup in the top bowl of a double boiler over medium-low heat. Heat until the chocolate is nearly melted, then stir with a heat-proof spatula or wooden spoon to combine. Use immediately or cover and refrigerate for up to 1 week, reheating before serving.

HOT FUDGE WITH HONEY

MAKES 1½ CUPS

While our hot fudge is sweetened with corn syrup, which leaves a pure chocolate taste, this sauce takes on a little more complexity. The nuances in our Mexican honey come through in a really nice way when warmed with chocolate and cream.

9 ounces semisweet chocolate, chopped

¾ cup heavy cream

¼ cup good-quality honey, preferably Mexican (see sidebar, page 29)

Combine the chocolate, cream, and honey in the top bowl of a double boiler over medium-low heat. Heat until the chocolate is nearly melted, then stir with a heat-proof spatula or wooden spoon to combine. Use immediately or cover and refrigerate for up to 1 week, reheating before serving.

WHITE CHOCOLATE BUTTERSCOTCH
WITH BANANAS

MAKES ABOUT 3 CUPS

We took an old-fashioned butterscotch recipe and added a little white chocolate. The result? The white chocolate softens the bitterness of the caramel and brings a luscious creamy texture to the sauce. Bananas make the perfect partner, but if you don't have any ripe ones around, you can leave them out. Serve this over ice cream, pound cake, or sliced fruit. Or eat it directly off the spoon!

½ cup sugar

1 cup plus 2 tablespoons heavy cream

1 pound plus 2 ounces finely chopped white chocolate (see Blue Ribbon Wisdom, page 150)

2 bananas, diced

1   In a heavy skillet, combine the sugar and 2 tablespoons water over medium heat. Cook, tilting the pan occasionally so that the sugar cooks evenly, until the sugar turns golden brown, about 5 minutes. Remove from the heat and let darken to a deep, nutty brown.

2   Carefully pour in the cream (it will splatter). Return the sauce to the heat and cook, stirring, until the sugar melts again and the mixture is smooth. Bring to a simmer.

3   Put the white chocolate in a large heat-proof bowl. Pour the hot cream mixture over the chocolate and stir until the sauce is smooth. Stir in the bananas and cook, stirring, until heated through. Keep covered in the refrigerator for up to 1 week and reheat to serve.

breakfast and brunch

◙ challah french toast with fresh berries and maple butter

◙ oatmeal–whole-wheat pancakes ◙ light and fluffy buttermilk

pancakes ◙ blueberry muffins ◙ baked blintz soufflé with

brown sugar bananas ◙ doughnut muffins ◙ maple scookies

◙ scrambled eggs with smoked trout and scallions

◙ the stanwich ◙ smoked salmon poached eggs ◙ blue

ribbon steak and eggs with red wine sauce ◙ chorizo and potato

hash ◙ blue benedict poached eggs ◙ breakfast salad with

fried egg, grilled shiitake mushroom, and fennel ◙ homemade

challah bread ◙ raisin walnut bread ◙ country white bread

ven in the days before we were owners of a restaurant that's in oper-
ation from four P.M. to four A.M., we tended to keep pretty late hours.
As a result, we've always been in love with the whole notion of
brunch. A meal that can accommodate those who get up with the roost-
ers as well as those who need to catch up on their shut-eye? Brilliant.

Some brunch lovers favor sweets for the morning dish. Our Challah
French Toast with Fresh Berries and Maple Butter (page 172) and Baked
Blintz Soufflé with Brown Sugar Bananas (page 179) are for them. If you
have more of a salty, savory palate, or if you prefer to break your fast
later in the day, we offer Smoked Salmon Poached Eggs (page 191) or
Blue Ribbon Steak and Eggs with Red Wine Sauce (page 194). These are
among a slew of hearty brunch favorites we serve at Blue Ribbon that
keep our customers lingering at the table for hours—although the bloody
Marys and mimosas probably have something to do with that, too.

For the days when we have more strenuous activities planned (we
do get out of the kitchen every now and then), we created lighter brunch
fare such as The Stanwich (page 188), based on a breakfast brainstorm
from Suzanne's husband, the eponymous Stan, and our famous Breakfast Salad with Fried Egg, Grilled Shiitake Mushroom, and Fennel (page
199), the perfect start to a day for the Blue Ribbon Cycling Team (yes,
there really is one of those).

Or, if you're really in a rush, just grab one of our perfect Blueberry
Muffins (page 178), Doughnut Muffins (page 182), or Maple Scookies
(page 185) to eat on the go. That's what's so spectacular about brunch:
the sheer volume of choices is staggering and each one is a winner.

CHALLAH FRENCH TOAST
WITH FRESH BERRIES AND MAPLE BUTTER

SERVES 4 TO 6

W e love to make French toast with challah because the bread is already so extrava-
gantly eggy, rich, and buttery that it adds a lot to the overall flavor of the dish,
and it soaks up the custard surprisingly well. For the fattest, most custardy and satiny
French toast, you need to get the bread to absorb as much of the egg mixture as possible before it saturates and falls apart (a dunk of about five minutes will do the trick).
Of course, you can still fry it up even if it does fall apart—it just won't look as pretty.
(If you serve it before everyone is caffeinated, they may not even notice.)

MAPLE BUTTER

8 tablespoons (1 stick) unsalted butter, at
    room temperature

2½ teaspoons pure maple syrup

FRENCH TOAST

6 large eggs

½ cup whole milk

¼ cup sugar

2 teaspoons vanilla extract

¼ teaspoon ground cinnamon

Pinch of salt

8 (1-inch) slices challah bread, homemade
    (page 000) or your favorite store-
    bought soft loaf

3 to 6 tablespoons unsalted butter, as
    needed

Fresh berries, such as blueberries,
    raspberries, or sliced strawberries,
    for serving

Confectioners' sugar, for serving

1 TO PREPARE THE MAPLE BUTTER: In a small bowl, beat together the softened butter
   with the syrup until smooth. Cover tightly and refrigerate if not using soon (it
   will keep for up to 1 week).

2 TO MAKE THE FRENCH TOAST: In a large bowl, whisk together the eggs, milk, sugar,
   vanilla, cinnamon, and salt. Pour the custard into a wide, shallow dish. Soak
   each slice of bread in the liquid, turning to coat on both sides, until the bread is
   saturated but not falling apart, 4 to 5 minutes.

recipe continues

3   Heat a large skillet over medium-high heat. Melt 1½ tablespoons of the butter in the pan. Working in batches, cook the challah until golden brown, 2 to 3 minutes per side. Repeat with the remaining challah, adding butter as needed.

4   Divide the toast among individual plates and serve, topped with maple butter, fresh berries, and a dusting of confectioners' sugar.

VARIATION ▣ CINNAMON SUGAR FRENCH TOAST

Omit the maple butter and berries. Combine ½ cup sugar with ½ tablespoon ground cinnamon in a small bowl. Divide the hot French toast among individual plates and top each slice with a fat pat of butter. Let the butter melt slightly, then sprinkle immediately and liberally with the cinnamon sugar.

VARIATION ▣ RAISIN WALNUT FRENCH TOAST WITH CINNAMON MAPLE BUTTER

If you eat a slice of our raisin walnut bread still warm from the oven, it's so cakelike, soft, and cinnamony that you can't help but think of turning it into French toast. Using this bread rather than challah will make for a firmer, sweeter, and spicier *pain perdu*, as the French say, with a more pronounced crust. So for crust lovers, this is your breakfast. When we were little, Bruce would never eat his crusts; he'd cut them all off and Eric would eat them. Eric was a big fan of the crusty outsides while Bruce loved the fluffy insides. That was kind of a jumping-off point for our culinary partnership. But we both love this French toast.

Add a pinch of ground cinnamon to the maple butter. Substitute Raisin Walnut Bread, homemade (page 202) or purchased for the challah.

OATMEAL–WHOLE-WHEAT PANCAKES

For this hearty breakfast recipe, we take our light-as-air buttermilk pancakes (page 177) and add whole-wheat flour and rolled oats for flavor and texture. Because the basic pancakes are already so airy, even whole grains won't weigh them down, meaning these are the most tender, melt-in-your-mouth whole-wheat pancakes you are ever going to make. We substitute brown sugar for regular granulated sugar because we like its intensity, and it goes nicely with the whole-wheat flour. Maple sugar would be terrific here, too.

1 cup all-purpose flour

¾ cup whole-wheat flour

¼ cup quick-cooking or instant oats

2 tablespoons light brown sugar

2 teaspoons baking powder

½ teaspoon baking soda

¼ teaspoon salt

2½ cups buttermilk

2 large eggs

2 tablespoons vegetable or canola oil

1½ tablespoons unsalted butter, plus more for serving

Pure maple syrup, for serving

1 In a large bowl, whisk together the flours, oats, brown sugar, baking powder, baking soda, and salt.

2 In a separate bowl, whisk together the buttermilk, eggs, and oil. Gradually stir the wet ingredients into the dry.

3 In a large skillet or on a griddle over medium-high heat, melt the butter. Working in batches, spoon ¼ cup pancake batter into the pan. Cook the pancakes until the edges have begun to brown and air bubbles form on each pancake's surface, about 3 minutes. Flip the pancakes and cook until golden, 1 to 2 minutes more. Serve hot, spread with butter and drizzled with maple syrup.

LIGHT AND FLUFFY BUTTERMILK PANCAKES

MAKES ABOUT 15 PANCAKES; SERVES 4 TO 6

These pancakes are based on the ones our partner Suzanne Allgair's mom always made when Suzanne was growing up. We've just increased the buttermilk to make them a little thinner, more ethereal, and crispier. Pancakes have been one of our all-time favorite cooking experiences ever since we were little kids. We always used a recipe from our mom's *Joy of Cooking* for something called "French Pancakes," which were basically crepes, and we used to make a game out of who could flip the thinnest one out of the pan without tearing it. We loved the translucent delicacy of those early flapjacks, and we've tried to reproduce that here, with the added fluffiness factor that separates the pancake from the crepe.

2 cups all-purpose flour

2 tablespoons sugar

2 teaspoons baking powder

½ teaspoon baking soda

¼ teaspoon salt

2½ cups buttermilk

2 large eggs

2 tablespoons vegetable or canola oil

1½ tablespoons unsalted butter, plus more for serving

Pure maple syrup, for serving

1   In a large bowl, whisk together the flour, sugar, baking powder, baking soda, and salt.

2   In a separate bowl, whisk together the buttermilk, eggs, and oil. Gradually stir the wet ingredients into the dry.

3   In a large skillet or on a griddle over medium-high heat, melt the butter. Working in batches, spoon ¼ cup pancake batter into the pan. Cook the pancakes until the edges have begun to brown and air bubbles form on each pancake's surface, about 3 minutes. Flip the pancakes and cook until golden, 1 to 2 minutes more. Serve hot, spread with butter and drizzled with maple syrup.

VARIATION ▣ BANANA PANCAKES

Fold 2 cups sliced fresh banana into the batter just before cooking.

BLUEBERRY MUFFINS

MAKES 12 MUFFINS

The appeal of muffins, for us, has always been that they provide a socially acceptable way to eat cake for breakfast. These are buoyant, finely textured, and very moist with just the right amount of blueberries.

2 cups all-purpose flour

2 teaspoons baking powder

1 teaspoon ground cinnamon

½ teaspoon salt

¼ teaspoon freshly ground nutmeg

½ cup sour cream, at room temperature

2 large eggs, lightly beaten, at room temperature

1 cup plus 2 tablespoons sugar

8 tablespoons (1 stick) unsalted butter, softened

2 cups fresh blueberries

1 Preheat the oven to 375°F. Grease a 12-cup muffin tin.

2 In a large bowl, sift together the flour, baking powder, cinnamon, salt, and nutmeg. In a separate bowl, whisk together the sour cream and eggs.

3 In the bowl of an electric mixer, beat together 1 cup of the sugar and the butter until creamy. Mix one quarter of the dry ingredients into the butter mixture. Beat in one third of the sour cream mixture. Continue to alternate until all of the remaining ingredients are incorporated, finishing with the dry ingredients. Do not overmix. Fold in the blueberries.

4 Fill the muffin cups two-thirds full with batter. Sprinkle the tops with the remaining 2 tablespoons sugar. Bake until golden on top and a toothpick inserted in the center of the muffins comes out clean, 20 to 25 minutes. Let cool for 5 minutes in the pan before serving or turning out onto a wire rack to cool completely.

BAKED BLINTZ SOUFFLÉ
WITH BROWN SUGAR BANANAS

We've always loved blintzes, having grown up on the outstanding made-from-scratch beauties from Grandma Martha's kitchen. She even let us help her make them, a big honor because blintzes were really her marquee dish. So when we were putting together a breakfast menu, it seemed natural to include some kind of blintz, amended with our own little twist. And that's how we go to this puffy pancake, which has all the sweet and tangy flavors of a blintz but is a bit more delicate and breakfast-like than the original. It's also a lot easier to put together; instead of making crepes and wrapping them around a filling, here we just top a hot, eggy, souffléd pancake (which is similar to a Dutch baby) with ricotta cream and syrupy brown sugar bananas. Serve this just as it emerges, puffed and steaming, from the oven. If you don't feel like making the brown sugar bananas, try topping the pancake with fresh berries and a drizzle of good honey. Or a simple dusting of confectioners' sugar and lemon juice is bright-tasting and sublime.

RICOTTA CREAM

1 cup fresh whole-milk ricotta cheese

1½ ounces cream cheese

2 tablespoons honey

Finely grated zest of 1 lemon

BLINTZ SOUFFLÉ

¾ cup all-purpose flour, sifted

⅓ cup granulated sugar

4 large eggs, at room temperature

1⅓ cups whole milk, at room temperature

8 tablespoons (1 stick) unsalted butter

BROWN SUGAR BANANAS

1 cup (packed) dark brown sugar

⅛ teaspoon kosher salt

½ cup plus 2 tablespoons sour cream

2 bananas, thinly sliced

1 teaspoon vanilla extract

I   Preheat the oven to 425°F.

2   TO MAKE THE RICOTTA CREAM: Combine the ricotta, cream cheese, honey, and lemon zest in a food processor and blend until smooth. Cover tightly with plastic wrap and chill until ready to use.

recipe continues

3   TO MAKE THE BLINTZ SOUFFLÉ: In a large bowl, whisk together the flour and granulated sugar. In a separate bowl, whisk together the eggs and milk. Gradually
stir the wet ingredients into the dry, whisking until the mixture is smooth.

4   Place the butter in the bottom of a shallow, 2-quart gratin dish or 9 × 12-inch
baking dish. Place the baking dish into the oven until the butter begins to bubble, 5 minutes.

5   Remove the dish from the oven; pour in the batter evenly. Return to the oven
and bake until the soufflé begins to rise and brown on the edges, about 17 minutes for a softer, more custardy texture and 20 to 25 minutes for a firmer, more
pancake-like result.

6   TO MAKE THE BANANAS: In a medium saucepan over medium heat, combine the
brown sugar, 2 tablespoons water, and the salt. Cook, stirring, until the sugar
is melted and the mixture is bubbling, about 5 minutes. Stir in the sour cream
and bananas; cook until heated through, 2 minutes more. Stir in the vanilla.

7   Add a dollop of the ricotta cream to the center of the pancake. Drizzle half the
banana mixture into the center of the cream. Slice and serve, with the remaining banana mixture on the side.

blue ribbon wisdom

IS IT DONE YET? There are several variables when it comes to
deciding if this soufflé is finished baking. A shorter stint in the oven
will give it an almost flanlike texture, which is delicious, though you
might notice butter separating from the custard and running down
the sides like a rich golden sauce. A longer bake time helps the
butter brown and soak into the soufflé, which takes on a firmer,
heartier texture. It's delicious both ways, so you really can't lose;
but don't be surprised by a certain amount of variation when you
make this.

DOUGHNUT MUFFINS

MAKES 24 MINI MUFFINS OR 12 MINI BUNDT CAKES

These have all the nutmegy goodness and dunk-ability of a traditional doughnut, but without the frying. We think they're even better baked than fried, because these have a delicious sourness from the buttermilk, a subtle flavor that gets lost in the deep-fryer. Once you've devoured these warm, brushed with a little melted butter and sprinkled with cinnamon sugar, you'll never yearn for doughnuts any other way. The batter will keep for three days in the fridge, so you can prepare it in advance and bake them up whenever a doughnut craving hits. And, if you just have to have a doughnut with a hole in the middle, you can bake them in mini Bundt pans.

MUFFINS

3 cups all-purpose flour

2½ teaspoons baking powder

¾ teaspoon salt

½ teaspoon freshly ground nutmeg

¼ teaspoon baking soda

¾ cup whole milk, at room temperature

2 tablespoons buttermilk, at room temperature

10 tablespoons (1¼ sticks) unsalted butter, at room temperature

¾ cup plus 2 tablespoons sugar

2 large eggs, at room temperature

COATING

1 cup sugar

1 tablespoon ground cinnamon

8 tablespoons (1 stick) unsalted butter, melted

1 Preheat the oven to 375°F. Grease and flour 2 (12-cup) mini muffin tins.

2 TO MAKE THE MUFFINS: In a bowl, sift together the flour, baking powder, salt, nutmeg, and baking soda. In a separate bowl, whisk together the milk and buttermilk.

3 In the bowl of an electric mixer fitted with the paddle attachment, beat the butter and sugar until light and fluffy. Beat in the eggs, one at a time, until just combined.

4 With the mixer set on low speed, beat in one fourth of the dry ingredients. Beat in one third of the milk mixture. Continue to alternate until all of the remaining ingredients are incorporated, finishing with the dry ingredients. Do not overmix.

5 Fill the prepared muffin cups just to the rim with batter. Bake until lightly golden and firm to the touch, 15 to 20 minutes. Let the muffins cool in the pan for 5 minutes. Remove the muffins from the tins and transfer to a wire rack set over a baking sheet.

6 TO COAT THE MUFFINS: Combine the sugar and cinnamon in a bowl. Brush each muffin generously with melted butter. Then sprinkle generously with cinnamon sugar. Serve warm or at room temperature.

VARIATION ▣ JELLY DOUGHNUT MUFFINS

If jelly doughnuts are more your style, allow the muffins to cool and use a small pastry tip to make a hole in the bottom of each muffin. Fill the pastry bag with your favorite jam, jelly, or citrus curd, and squeeze into the muffin.

MAPLE SCOOKIES

We came up with this recipe after a failed attempt at making what we hoped would be the world's best scones. Instead, we got buttery, rich, cookie-like pastries with a deep maple taste. They weren't quite sweet enough to qualify as true cookies, but they were crisper and thinner than a scone. So we dubbed them scookies. Now we like them even better than regular scones.

SCOOKIES

3 cups all-purpose flour

¼ cup (packed) dark brown sugar

1½ teaspoons baking powder

½ teaspoon baking soda

½ teaspoon salt

12 tablespoons (1½ sticks) unsalted butter, chilled and cut into ½-inch pieces

½ cup whipping cream

½ cup pure maple syrup

GLAZE

⅔ cup confectioners' sugar

2 tablespoons pure maple syrup

4 to 6 tablespoons heavy cream

1   Preheat the oven to 350°F. Line a baking sheet with parchment paper.

2   To make the scookies: In a large bowl, whisk together the flour, brown sugar, baking powder, baking soda, and salt. Cut in the butter until it resembles a coarse meal.

3   In a bowl, stir together the cream and syrup. Gradually stir this mixture into the flour until it just comes together. Turn the dough out onto a lightly floured surface. Knead gently for about five turns. Divide the dough in half and form each into a 2-inch-thick circle, about 8 inches in diameter. Cut each round into 8 equal wedges.

4   Transfer the wedges to the lined baking sheet 2 inches apart and bake until golden brown on top, 15 to 25 minutes.

5   In a small bowl, whisk together the confectioners' sugar, syrup, and just enough cream to make a thick glaze, with a consistency slightly thicker than molasses. (It should be thick enough to mound up when you drop it from a spoon.) Spoon the glaze over the hot scookies and transfer to a wire rack to cool.

SCRAMBLED EGGS
WITH SMOKED TROUT AND SCALLIONS

SERVES 4

This dish packs a taste wallop. The trout imparts a lingering salty, smoky character that's almost like bacon, but fishy, in a good way, and it melds beautifully with eggs and scallions. The cooked scallions in the eggs turn golden and sweet, providing a nice contrast to the fresh, green, oniony vibrancy of the raw scallions sprinkled on top and to the spiciness of the hot sauce. For so few ingredients, the dish is complex, even transcendent. It's scrambled eggs in their finest form.

8 large eggs

Pinch of salt

2 dashes of hot sauce

2 tablespoons unsalted butter, plus more for serving

4 ounces smoked trout, sliced into ¼-inch strips

½ cup thinly sliced scallions, green and white parts

Toasted rye or multigrain bread, for serving

1   In a large bowl, whisk together the eggs, salt, and hot sauce until slightly frothy.

2   Heat the butter in a medium skillet over low heat. Add the smoked trout and half the scallions. Cook, stirring, for 30 seconds. Add the eggs. Once the eggs have begun to very lightly set, begin to stir them gently using a heat-proof rubber spatula. Make sure to scrape all edges of the pan. Continue this process until the eggs are creamy and just cooked through, about 2 minutes. Divide among serving plates and garnish with the remaining ¼ cup scallions. Serve, with slices of buttered toasted rye or multigrain bread.

blue ribbon wisdom

PERFECT SCRAMBLED EGGS

- Of course, you want to use the best quality eggs possible. If you can get good, farm-fresh eggs from a farmer's market or from a friend with a chicken, you may not need to use any additional seasoning.
- Use a nonstick skillet. You won't have to worry about your eggs sticking to the pan.
- The fat you add to the skillet is really important, as it will impart its flavor to the eggs. For fluffy buttery eggs, use high-fat, unsalted European butter. For a lighter dish, use your best-quality extra-virgin olive oil.
- The key to good scrambled eggs is to not use high heat, which will lead to dried-out eggs. Use medium to low heat and stir constantly, trying to incorporate the eggs from the sides of the pan into the center.
- For especially fluffy scrambled eggs that are terrific served naked, add 1 ice cube for every 2 eggs. The steam from the melting ice makes the eggs especially light-textured. Drop the ice into the pan along with the eggs, and lightly stir with a heat-proof spatula or fork until the eggs just come together to form a light, soft scrambled egg.
- Take the skillet off of the heat just before the eggs are done. They will finish cooking in the pan perfectly.

THE STANWICH

Our partner Suzanne Allgair's husband, Stan, kept talking about this fantastic, revolutionary egg concept he had that was going to turn the breakfast world on its head. Sure enough, he was really onto something. His big idea was to make a spicy, scrambled-egg-and-cheddar sandwich on our bacon and grilled onion flatbread. Ever since the day we finally tried it, it's become a mainstay among staff and customers alike. Here, we simplified the recipe to call for purchased ciabatta, which is easier than making your own flatbread. But if you feel like baking bread, go ahead and substitute the flatbread on page 40. Either way, it's a great combination that truly lives up to all of Stan's hype.

2 slices bacon

1 large ciabatta loaf, halved horizontally and cut crosswise into quarters

Perfect Sauté Seasoning (page 251) or salt and freshly ground white or black pepper

1½ tablespoons extra-virgin olive oil

1 red onion, sliced ¼ inch thick

8 large eggs

Several dashes of hot sauce

2 tablespoons unsalted butter

1 cup (4 ounces) grated aged cheddar cheese

1 In a medium skillet over medium-high heat, cook the bacon until crisp, 3 to 5 minutes. Transfer the bacon to a paper-towel-lined plate. Reserve the pan fat.

2 Preheat the broiler.

3 Place the 8 pieces of bread cut side up on a baking sheet. Drizzle with the bacon fat and season lightly.

4 Heat the oil in a grill pan or skillet over high heat until hot, but not smoking. Grill or sear the onions with a pinch of seasoning until charred and tender, 5 to 7 minutes, turning once. Crumble in the bacon.

recipe continues

5 In a large bowl, whisk together the eggs, a pinch of seasoning, and the hot sauce until slightly frothy. Melt the butter in a nonstick or other skillet. Add the eggs and sprinkle with the cheese. Once the eggs have begun to very lightly set, begin to stir them gently using a heat-proof rubber spatula. Make sure to scrape all edges of the pan. Continue this process until the eggs are creamy and just cooked through, about 2 minutes. Remove from the heat and cover.

6 Broil the bread until lightly toasted, about 1 minute (watch closely to see that it does not burn). Divide 4 slices of bread among 4 serving plates. Place some of the scrambled eggs on each slice. Spoon the onion-bacon mixture over the eggs. Top with the remaining slices of bread.

VARIATION ▣ THE SUZANNEWICH

Stan's wife, Suzanne, loves this open-faced breakfast sandwich with chorizo and onions. To make it, sauté fresh chorizo sausage (removed from the casing) with some chopped yellow onion and a garlic clove or two. Top a slice of toasted country white bread with a fried egg (preferably over-easy), and sprinkle the top with the chorizo mixture and some greated Monterey Jack cheese. If you have tomatillo salsa or a julienned roasted poblano chile pepper on hand, add a little of that before sprinkling with the cheese. Place under the broiler until the cheese is melted, about 2 minutes.

SMOKED SALMON POACHED EGGS

SERVES 4

The sublime mix of salmon, caviar, and sour cream has found its way into many of our recipes over the years. We've loved the combination ever since the days when we used to take $1.99 supermarket Romanoff black caviar, stir it into sour cream, and eat it on toast. We thought we were living in the lap of luxury. And if you use good caviar and add smoked salmon, it's really heaven. The truth is, add smoked salmon and caviar to any dish and you'll have a guaranteed crowd-pleaser.

5 large eggs

Perfect Sauté Seasoning (page 251) or salt and freshly ground white or black pepper

1 ounce American sturgeon caviar

Hollandaise Sauce (page 238), warm

4 (½-inch-thick) slices rye bread, toasted

8 ounces smoked salmon

3 tablespoons brined capers, drained (optional)

3 tablespoons finely chopped red onion (optional)

Chopped fresh flat-leaf parsley leaves, for garnish (optional)

Fennel Slaw (page 234), for serving (optional)

1   Place 1 egg in a medium saucepan and fill the pan with water to cover. Bring the water to a boil over medium-high heat; reduce the heat and simmer for 5 minutes. Remove the egg with a slotted spoon and transfer to a bowl of ice water to cool. Peel and finely chop the egg.

2   Increase the heat of the cooking water so that it is at barely a simmer. Crack one of the remaining eggs into a teacup or ramekin. Use a spoon to stir the pot of simmering water, creating a swirl. Carefully slide the egg into the swirling water. Repeat with the remaining eggs. Continue stirring the water gently in one direction. Cook until the whites are firm and the yolks lightly set, 1 to 1½ minutes. Remove the eggs from the water with a slotted spoon. Place the eggs on a damp dish towel and season lightly.

3   Gently stir the caviar into the warm hollandaise.

recipe continues

4   To serve, divide the toast among individual serving plates. Place some salmon on each slice of toast and top with a poached egg. Drizzle with the caviar cream, and sprinkle each dish with hard-boiled egg, capers, red onion, and parsley, if desired. Serve, with fennel slaw alongside if you like.

blue ribbon wisdom

PERFECT POACHED EGGS Bruce's very first cooking job was in a restaurant in Colorado called Le Peep, where the day started at 5:30 in the morning and he was responsible for the poached eggs. Every day there were 600 eggs to cook, and he became incredibly intimate with the ins and outs of egg poaching that summer.

- Remember the fresher the egg, the better the white will hold together and surround the yolk when you poach it.
- Make sure the water is bubbling, but not at too rapid a speed, otherwise the egg white will shred when it first hits the water. A lively simmer is about right to help the egg hold together.
- Never add salt to the water; it will break down the white of the egg. Salting the water is a great way to make egg-drop soup, but not so great for perfect poached eggs.
- Adding a drop of vinegar to the poaching liquid will help the white stay solid and hold together.
- A shallow nonstick pan with just enough water to cover the yolk works really well for poaching, especially if you are cooking several eggs at a time. They're easier to keep track of in a shallow pan than a big deep one.
- Make a slow circular motion with the pan so the egg envelops itself with the white when you carefully slide it in.
- The biggest mistake people make with poaching is that they forget to drain the poaching water off the egg before serving. Sometimes water gets trapped in the white, which leaks onto the plate or bread, making it soggy and unpleasant. At the restaurant, we always put a damp kitchen towel on the counter and, using a slotted spoon, we hold the egg over the towel and give the spoon a few taps to shake off the moisture.

BLUE RIBBON STEAK AND EGGS
WITH RED WINE SAUCE

SERVES 4

This is another recipe inspired by restaurant Le Recamier's *oeufs en meurette*. The first time we saw it, we were stunned by the idea that eggs poached in red wine and served on toast qualified as an appetizer or lunch dish to the citizens of France. Back in the 1980s, *oeufs en meurette* was already old-fashioned, a Bungundian specialty that had peaked in popularity in the '50s and '60s, when it had been on bistro menus all over town. By the time we got to Paris, it was almost a relic, but a really tasty one.

Anyway, we took the idea of *oeufs en meurette* and combined it with the steak-and-egg breakfasts we used to eat in New Orleans at a chain called, not surprisingly, Steak 'N' Eggs Kitchen. Rare steak, eggs, and red wine sauce all on one plate—yum!

2 (10-ounce) New York strip steaks, about 1¼ inches thick

1½ tablespoons extra-virgin olive oil

Perfect Sauté Seasoning (page 251) or salt and freshly ground white or black pepper

Red Wine Sauce (page 236)

4 large eggs

Chopped fresh flat-leaf parsley leaves, for garnish

Crispy Taters (page 126) or Oven-Crisped Potatoes (page 124), for serving

1 Bring a medium saucepan of water barely to a simmer over medium heat. Keep at a steady simmer over low heat.

2 Place the steaks on a large plate; coat with oil and sprinkle with seasoning. Heat a heavy skillet over medium-high heat until very hot, but not smoking. Place the steaks in the pan and sear, without moving, until dark golden, 4 to 5 minutes per side for medium-rare. Transfer to a platter to rest.

3 Bring the wine sauce to a simmer over medium-low heat.

4 Crack an egg into a teacup or ramekin. Use a spoon to stir the pan of simmering water, creating a swirl. Carefully slide the egg into the swirling water. Repeat with the remaining eggs. Continue stirring the water gently in one direction. Cook until the whites are firm and the yolks lightly set, 1 to 1½ minutes.

recipe continues

Remove the eggs from the water with a slotted spoon. Place the eggs on a damp dish towel and season lightly.

5   To serve, slice the steak on the bias into ⅛-inch-thick slices and divide among 4 serving plates. Place a poached egg on top of the steak, and drizzle with wine sauce. Garnish with parsley. Serve immediately, with the potatoes.

CHORIZO AND POTATO HASH

SERVES 4

The first time we ever had hash was when we went with our dad to a fishing camp in Maine. We slept in a cabin, which was a generous name for it, and the only food available since we utterly failed at the fly-fishing was cans of corned-beef hash. Right there we decided it was the best thing we'd ever tasted in our lives. Since then we've been obsessed with making hash for breakfast. We hit upon this version because we happened to have some chorizo lying around the kitchen, and jalapeños add a nice kick. Serve it with your favorite kind of eggs.

1 large onion, peeled and diced

1½ tablespoons extra-virgin olive oil

Perfect Sauté Seasoning (page 251) or salt and freshly ground white or black pepper

6 ounces dried chorizo, cut into ¼-inch pieces

3 tablespoons chopped pickled jalapeños

1 garlic clove, minced

Crispy Taters (page 126) or Oven-Crisped Potatoes (page 124)

¼ teaspoon hot paprika

Chopped fresh cilantro leaves, for garnish

1   In a large skillet over medium heat, combine the onion, oil, and a pinch of seasoning. Cook, stirring occasionally, until softened, about 5 minutes. Stir in the chorizo, jalapeños, and garlic, and cook for 2 minutes more.

2   Increase the heat to medium-high. Add the potatoes and paprika and toss to combine; cook for 2 minutes more. Garnish with cilantro and serve.

BLUE BENEDICT POACHED EGGS

Everybody loves classic eggs Benedict, so it was a challenge to make the dish interesting and fresh. We kept trying to make homemade English muffins and they never turned out as well as we wanted. So we decided to play to our strength and use our own terrific challah instead. The eggy sweetness of the bread makes for an excellent combination with the saltiness of Serrano ham and Jarlsberg cheese, and the acidity of tomato. If you want, omit the eggs and top this with another piece of challah to make the greatest grilled cheese Monte Cristo you've ever had.

4 (¾-inch-thick) slices challah bread, homemade (page 200) or your favorite store-bought soft loaf

3 ounces sliced Serrano ham

1 medium tomato, cored and very thinly sliced

2 cups (8 ounces) grated Jarlsberg or other Swiss-style cheese

8 large eggs

Perfect Sauté Seasoning (page 251) or salt and freshly ground white or black pepper

Hollandaise Sauce (page 238), warm

Chopped fresh flat-leaf parsley leaves, for garnish

1 Preheat the broiler. Arrange an oven rack 4 inches from the heat. Bring a medium saucepan of water barely to a simmer.

2 Place the challah slices in a single layer on a baking sheet. Top each slice with a layer of ham, followed by a layer of tomato. Cover evenly with cheese. Broil until the bread is golden and the cheese is melted and bubbling, 1 to 2 minutes (watch carefully to see that they do not burn).

3 Crack an egg into a teacup or ramekin. Use a spoon to stir the pot of simmering water, creating a swirl. Carefully slide the egg into the swirling water. Repeat with the remaining eggs. Continue stirring the water gently in one direction. Cook until the whites are firm and the yolks lightly set, 1 to 1½ minutes. Remove the eggs from the water with a slotted spoon. Place the eggs on a damp dish towel and season lightly.

4 Place hot slices of baked challah on individual serving plates. Top each with 2 poached eggs, warm hollandaise sauce, and parsley.

BREAKFAST SALAD
WITH FRIED EGG, GRILLED SHIITAKE MUSHROOM, AND FENNEL

SERVES 4

This breakfast salad is a riff on a traditional poached egg French salad. The hot yolk emulsifies with the lemon and olive oil in a light dressing, which coats the greens while simultaneously wilting them. It is just the kind of delicious, clean meal that makes everyone happy and ready to attack the day.

¼ cup plus 1½ tablespoons extra-virgin olive oil

6 ounces shiitake mushrooms (2 cups)

Perfect Sauté Seasoning (page 251) or salt and freshly ground white or black pepper

2 cups watercress

2 cups baby greens

½ small fennel bulb, quartered, cored, and very thinly sliced lengthwise

1 ounce grated Parmigiano-Reggiano cheese, plus more for serving

2 tablespoons freshly squeezed lemon juice

3 tablespoons unsalted butter

8 large eggs

1 Preheat the grill, or heat a grill pan over high heat until very hot, but not smoking.

2 In a bowl, toss together 1½ tablespoons of the oil with the mushrooms. Grill the mushrooms, cap side down, and sprinkle them lightly with seasoning. Cook, turning once, until golden brown, about 5 minutes.

3 Transfer the mushrooms to a plate to cool. In a large bowl, toss together the watercress, greens, fennel, and cheese. In a small bowl, whisk together the lemon juice and a pinch of seasoning. Whisk in the remaining ¼ cup oil. Toss enough of the vinaigrette into the salad to lightly coat the greens; divide among 4 individual serving plates.

4 In a large skillet over medium heat, melt 1½ tablespoons of the butter. Working in two batches, crack 4 eggs into the skillet and sprinkle with seasoning. Cook the eggs over medium-low heat until the whites are set, about 5 minutes. Place 2 eggs on each of 2 plates. Repeat with the remaining butter and eggs. Top the eggs with the mushrooms and more grated cheese for serving.

HOMEMADE CHALLAH BREAD

MAKES 2 BRAIDED LOAVES OR 1 DOZEN HAMBURGER BUNS (SEE VARIATION)

As kids, we would visit our grandmother in Clifton, New Jersey, on Friday nights. And the most significant, most special part of the visit would be when she'd take us to the Allwood Bakery to pick up the challah bread for the night's meal. We'd go into the bakery and pick out the bread, either plain or with raisins. Usually it was braided, except on Rosh Hashanah, when it was round. To our grandma, the challah was sacred. You could see it in the way she'd handle the loaf, like a cherished newborn. Later at the evening meal, we couldn't wait to pray over and cut up that challah, and bite into its fluffy, egg-rich sweetness. When we opened Blue Ribbon Bakery, our first objective was to make a challah bread that was as good as the ones from our memory.

1⅓ ounces fresh yeast or 1 teaspoon active dry yeast

5 large eggs

5⅓ cups bread flour

⅔ cup sugar

1 tablespoon plus 2 teaspoons kosher salt

2 cups (4 sticks) butter, cubed, at room temperature

Nonstick cooking spray

1 In the bowl of an electric mixer with a hook attachment, combine the yeast with 1 cup lukewarm water until the yeast dissolves. Crack 4 of the eggs into the bowl and mix just until the eggs break up.

2 Add the flour, sugar, and salt and mix until a stiff dough comes together, 3 to 5 minutes. While the mixer is running, add the butter cube by cube. Mix the dough for 10 to 15 minutes more until it completely pulls away from the side of the bowl and has a glossy appearance.

3 Lightly grease a large bowl with nonstick cooking spray. Gently knead the dough into a ball and place it in the bowl. Lightly grease a sheet of plastic wrap and loosely cover the dough, greased side down. Allow the dough to rise until tripled in size, at least 1 hour and up to 2 hours.

4 Preheat the oven to 375°F. Line 2 baking sheets with parchment paper.

5 Gently punch down the dough and separate it into 6 equal pieces of about 9 ounces each. Take 3 of the dough pieces and roll them into ropes about 8 inches in length. Tightly braid the 3 ropes of dough and place the loaf on a baking sheet. Repeat with the remaining dough pieces to make a second loaf and place it on the other baking sheet. Lightly grease 2 sheets of plastic wrap. Cover the loaves with the plastic, greased side down, and let rise for at least 20 minutes and up to 30 minutes, or until the dough begins to get visibly puffy.

6 Crack the remaining egg into a small bowl and lightly beat. Brush the egg wash over the loaves, being sure to hit the cracks between the braids.

7 Bake for 35 to 40 minutes, or until the loaves are a uniform golden brown and they sound hollow when tapped. Transfer to a wire rack to cool.

VARIATION ▣ CHALLAH HAMBURGER BUNS

When the dough is ready to shape, divide it into 12 equal pieces (about 5 ounces each). Using the cupped palm of your hand, roll each piece into a tight ball. Transfer to 2 baking sheets and let rise, covered with greased plastic wrap, for at least 20 minutes and up to 30 minutes. Brush the buns with egg wash and bake for 25 to 30 minutes, or until the buns are a uniform golden brown and sound hollow when tapped. Transfer to a wire rack to cool.

RAISIN WALNUT BREAD

This is our variation on traditional date nut bread. It's slightly less sweet. It's terrific made into grilled cheese sandwiches, or just toasted and slathered with good butter. And we should note, it makes some of the best French toast ever (see page 172).

1⅛ teaspoons active dry yeast or 2 ounces fresh yeast

3 large eggs, lightly beaten

⅓ cup granulated sugar

¼ cup (packed) dark brown sugar

¼ cup honey

5¾ cups bread flour

2 teaspoons kosher salt

1½ teaspoons ground cinnamon

8 tablespoons (1 stick) unsalted butter, cubed, at room temperature

2 cups raisins

½ cup chopped walnuts

Nonstick cooking spray

1 In the bowl of an electric mixer with a hook attachment, combine the yeast with 1½ cups lukewarm water. Let the mixture stand at room temperature until it starts to foam, about 10 minutes.

2 Add the eggs, both sugars, and honey and mix for several seconds to combine. Add the flour gradually, mixing on medium speed until the dough starts to come together. Sprinkle in the salt and cinnamon and continue mixing.

3 Add the butter, cube by cube, and continue mixing. Once it is fully incorporated, about 10 minutes, add the raisins and walnuts and mix until combined.

4 Lightly grease a large bowl with nonstick cooking spray. Form the dough into a loose ball and place it in the bowl. Grease plastic wrap and cover the dough loosely. Allow the dough to rise until doubled in size, 1½ to 2 hours.

5 Preheat the oven to 375°F. Lightly grease a 9 × 4-inch loaf pan.

6 Punch down the dough, form it into a loaf, and place it in the prepared pan. Cover it loosely with the plastic and let it rest until puffed up to the rim of the pan, about 30 minutes. Uncover and bake for 50 minutes to 1 hour, or until the top is a dark golden brown and the loaf sounds hollow when tapped. Allow the bread to cool in the pan for 5 minutes before turning out onto a wire cooling rack.

COUNTRY WHITE BREAD

MAKES 2 (9 X 5-INCH) LOAVES

Our mom used to buy Arnold's Brick Oven bread from the supermarket. It came in a bag that had a drawing of Arnold, presumably, pulling out a glowing loaf from a stone oven. That's the image we had in our minds when we were creating country white bread in our own brick oven. The recipe draws on all our training in France, but the impetus to come up with it was straight outta the Jersey 'burbs.

1⅛ teaspoons active dry yeast or
  2 ounces fresh yeast

4½ cups bread flour

1 tablespoon kosher salt

Nonstick cooking spray

1 In the bowl of an electric mixer with a hook attachment, combine the yeast with 1¾ cups lukewarm water. Let stand until foamy, about 10 minutes.

2 Add 2 cups of the flour and mix for several seconds on low speed, then add the remaining 2½ cups flour and the salt. Mix on medium speed until the dough comes away from the sides of the bowl and forms a ball, about 10 minutes.

3 Lightly grease a large bowl with nonstick cooking spray. Form the dough into a loose ball and place it the bowl. Lightly grease a sheet of plastic wrap and loosely cover the dough, greased side down. Allow the dough to rise until nearly doubled in size, about 1 hour.

4 Punch down the dough, and knead for several turns. Form the dough into a ball, cover with the plastic wrap, and let rise until doubled for another hour.

5 Preheat the oven to 375°F. Lightly dust a workspace with flour and turn out the dough. Divide in half and shape each portion into a loaf by gently tucking it into itself until the outside is smooth. Lightly grease 2 (9 × 5-inch) loaf pans. Place the dough into the pans and let it rest, covered with a kitchen towel, for 30 minutes.

6 Bake for 1 hour, or until the tops of the bread are golden brown and the loaves sound hollow when tapped. Cool in the pans for 5 minutes before turning out onto a rack.

sandwiches

◉ mom's egg salad sandwich ◉ grilled eggplant sandwich

with cacio de roma cheese, tomato, and watercress

◉ shrimp salad sandwich with roasted tomato mayonnaise

◉ fried catfish sandwich on ciabatta with corn tartar sauce

◉ yellowfin tuna salad sandwich on toasted challah

◉ duck club sandwich ◉ grilled steak sandwich with

horseradish cream ◉ barbecued pork sandwich ◉ blt on

whole-wheat toast ◉ the blue reuben sandwich

The sandwich is definitely not just for lunch anymore. From our first grilled cheese made in Mom's trusty GE toaster oven, the pastrami on rye we'd get at the Morristown Deli, or the best muffuletta you can only get in the French Quarter of good old New Orleans, it became clear to us at an early age that nothing could satisfy on a deeper level than a sandwich. That's why they're found in lunch boxes, delis, sub joints, Parisian cafés, Arabian bazaars, Vietnamese markets, and on every menu we've ever written (breakfast and dinner menus included). It just goes to show that the world's fascination with two slices of bread flanking meat, cheese, vegetables, and endless concoctions of dressing, sauces, or mayo is showing no sign of waning.

With simple recipes like these, everything matters. To toast or not to toast, mayo or mustard, layered or stacked—all the details add up. We like to take classic sandwiches, such as the ubiquitous tuna salad or club sandwich, and heighten the quality of ingredients until we come up with a true masterpiece. We think we've achieved just such a work of art with our Yellowfin Tuna Salad Sandwich on Toasted Challah (page 215), made with fresh tuna fillets and saline capers, and our Duck Club Sandwich (page 216), made with succulent Muscovy duck breast, crispy bacon, and our extra-special homemade Raisin Walnut Bread (page 202).

Then we have the sandwiches that don't need to be dressed up because we love them just the way they are: Mom's Egg Salad Sandwich (page 208) or BLT on Whole-Wheat Toast (page 221).

Naturally, some of our kitchen experiments have found their way into this chapter. One of our favorites is the Barbecued Pork Sandwich (page 219). We've been snacking on that in the oven room of Blue Ribbon Bakery since we first opened. Now that is one sandwich we want to sit down for, but somehow we are compelled to consume it faster than we can make it to a chair! That's pretty much our definition of a great meal.

MOM'S EGG SALAD SANDWICH

MAKES 4 SANDWICHES

The state of New Jersey might not immediately spring to mind as a hotbed of culinary inspiration, but for us it was a virtual gold mine. The idea behind this sandwich came to us from memories of an amazing deli in Jersey called Tabatchnick's. We used to go there with our dad and we'd always get the same thing: creamy egg salad sandwiches served with a half-sour pickle that they'd pull out of a huge barrel and slap on the side of the plate. Our mom made a similar version at home. What's so special about her sandwich is that it's completely simple; she gives all the ingredients a rough chop so the egg whites stay in chunks surrounded by creamy yolk.

8 large eggs

½ cup finely chopped celery

½ cup Olive Oil Mayonnaise (page 240) or regular mayonnaise, plus more if needed

¼ teaspoon salt

Freshly ground white or black pepper

8 (¼-inch-thick) slices Country White Bread (page 203) or your favorite store-bought crusty loaf

Thinly sliced red onion, for serving

Tomato slices, for serving

Garlic Dill Pickles (page 228), cut into wedges, for serving

1 Place the eggs in a medium saucepan and fill with cold water to cover. Bring to a boil over high heat. Immediately remove the pan from the heat, cover, and let stand for 10 minutes. Drain the eggs, then plunge in ice water to cool. Peel the cooled eggs and roughly chop.

2 In a bowl, combine the eggs, celery, mayonnaise, salt, and a few grinds of pepper. If the salad seems dry, add more mayonnaise to reach the desired consistency. Taste and adjust the seasoning, if necessary.

3 Divide the filling among the slices of bread. Sandwich the bread slices together. Serve with onion, tomato, and pickle wedges on the side.

GRILLED EGGPLANT SANDWICH
WITH CACIO DE ROMA CHEESE, TOMATO, AND WATERCRESS

MAKES 4 SANDWICHES

The mild saltiness and creaminess of this nutty sheep's-milk cheese is a revelation. When it's melted, its texture is creamy but not gooey, and it partners perfectly with smoky grilled eggplant, fresh tomatoes, and watercress. If you can't find it, substitute any semi-firm, mild cheese, preferably made from sheep's milk.

8 (¼-inch-thick) eggplant rounds

2 tablespoons extra-virgin olive oil, plus more for drizzling

Perfect Sauté Seasoning (page 251) or salt and freshly ground white or black pepper

4 (5-ounce) ciabatta rolls, halved horizontally

16 slices Cacio de Roma or other semi-firm cheese such as gouda (about 8 ounces)

3 small tomatoes, thinly sliced

1 bunch of watercress

1   Preheat the oven to 400°F. Preheat a grill or grill pan until very hot.

2   Toss the eggplant with the oil and sprinkle with seasoning. Grill the eggplant until charred and tender, 2 to 3 minutes per side.

3   Drizzle the bread with oil and season lightly. Grill until crisp and light golden, 1 to 2 minutes per side.

4   Arrange the bread, cut side up, on a baking sheet. Layer the cheese on each slice of bread. Layer the bottom slices with tomato slices; layer the top slices with eggplant. Bake until the cheese is warm and melted, about 5 minutes. Arrange the watercress over the sandwiches and press the top and bottom bread halves together. Serve hot.

SHRIMP SALAD SANDWICH
WITH ROASTED TOMATO MAYONNAISE

This sandwich came about when we were toying with the idea of putting a lobster roll on the menu. The recipe took a turn, veering from one crustacean to another when we decided on shrimp salad instead. Then, once we started thinking about shrimp, we immediately remembered the fantastic shrimp Louis that our dad learned to make in San Francisco. It's basically just a combination of delicate bay shrimp coated with thousand island dressing. So we did a little riff, substituting roasted tomato mayo for the dressing, and it's proved very popular, especially with the substitution of jumbo shrimp.

24 jumbo shrimp (1¼ to 1½ pounds), peeled and deveined

Roasted Tomato Mayonnaise (page 240)

6 tablespoons finely chopped celery

1 teaspoon freshly squeezed lemon juice

Salt and freshly ground black pepper

8 (¼-inch-thick) slices challah bread, homemade (page 200) or your favorite store-bought soft loaf, toasted

Drained brined capers, for serving

Finely chopped red onion, for serving

Lemon wedges, for serving

Mixed greens, for serving

1 In a covered steamer basket set over a pot of simmering water, steam the shrimp until opaque, about 3 minutes; cool completely, then slice in half lengthwise.

2 In a bowl, combine the shrimp, tomato mayonnaise, celery, lemon juice, and salt and pepper to taste. Divide the shrimp salad among four slices of challah. Sprinkle with capers and red onion, then top with the remaining slices of bread. Serve the sandwiches with lemon wedges and mixed greens.

FRIED CATFISH SANDWICH
ON CIABATTA WITH CORN TARTAR SAUCE

MAKES 6 SANDWICHES

This recipe is inspired by the time Eric spent in New Orleans back in his college days at Tulane University. Fried fish po'boys were bar-food staples, and he certainly visited plenty of bars! The corn tartar sauce is unusual and works really well with the fish. It's our Southern USA twist on a classic French *sauce gribiche*, which relies on tiny cornichon pickles for a piquant flavor. In our sauce, the cornichons play nicely with the sweet corn. If you don't have ciabatta, use any crusty rolls or bread.

CORN TARTAR SAUCE

½ cup corn kernels (from 1 ear of fresh corn; see Blue Ribbon Wisdom)

1 cup Olive Oil Mayonnaise (page 240) or regular mayonnaise

¼ cup chopped red onion

2 tablespoons chopped cornichon pickles

1½ teaspoons cornichon pickling liquid

1 teaspoon Blue Ribbon Hot Sauce (page 242) or other hot sauce, or to taste

¾ teaspoon freshly squeezed lemon juice

¼ teaspoon Zatarain's crab boil (see Note)

CATFISH

Vegetable oil, for frying

1½ cups all-purpose flour

⅛ teaspoon baking powder

6 (6- to 7-ounce) catfish fillets

½ cup milk

Salt and freshly ground black pepper

2 cups shredded iceberg lettuce

6 (5-ounce) ciabatta or other crusty rolls, halved horizontally, soft centers pulled out and reserved for another use

Blue Ribbon Hot Sauce (page 242) or other hot sauce, to taste

1 large tomato, sliced

1 red onion, sliced

1 TO MAKE THE CORN TARTAR SAUCE: In a medium saucepan with a lid, set a steamer basket over an inch of water and bring to a boil. Add the corn, cover, and steam for 30 seconds. Let cool.

2 Put the mayonnaise in a bowl. Fold in the corn and the chopped onion, pickles, pickling liquid, hot sauce, lemon juice, and crab boil. Cover and refrigerate until ready to use, or up to 2 days.

recipe continues

3   TO MAKE THE FISH: Heat 2 inches of oil in a deep-sided skillet until it reaches 375°F. A piece of bread (such as a nugget of the soft center of a ciabatta) dropped into the oil will sizzle and quickly turn golden around the edges when the oil is at the correct temperature.

4   While the oil is heating, whisk together the flour and baking powder in a shallow dish. Using a sharp knife, score each fish fillet along the center of its skin side. Dip the fish fillets first into the milk, letting any excess drip off, and then into the flour mixture.

5   Carefully drop 1 fish fillet into the hot oil and fry until golden brown, 4 to 6 minutes. Drain on a paper-towel-lined plate, seasoning the fish with salt and pepper immediately. Repeat with the remaining fish fillets.

6   To serve, pile the lettuce into the scooped-out center of each roll's bottom half and top with the fish. Season with hot sauce. Top with corn tartar sauce, lettuce, tomato, and red onion. Cover with the ciabatta tops.

NOTE   Zatarain's crab boil is available at many supermarkets, and online (see Sources, page 252). Or, to make your own crab boil, in a small bowl combine ¼ cup Old Bay seasoning, 2 tablespoons cayenne, and 2 tablespoons salt. Store in an airtight container in a cool, dry place.

blue ribbon wisdom

FRESH CORN KERNELS   Here's how to slice the kernels off a fresh ear of corn in the least messy way we know. Hold an ear of corn upright in a large, deep bowl and slide a thin, flexible knife along the cob from the top to the middle, cutting the kernels off into the bowl. Turn the ear around and slice off the rest of the kernels in the same way.

YELLOWFIN TUNA SALAD SANDWICH
ON TOASTED CHALLAH

MAKES 4 SANDWICHES

Our mom was probably not alone in serving her kids what seemed like thousands of tuna salad sandwiches over the course of our childhood. We think it was her favorite thing to make for us. But it was years before we put it together that the tuna that came out of the can and got mixed with mayonnaise was the same tuna that's a fish. So we decided to take the best of both worlds: make a Mom-worthy classic tuna salad from top-quality fresh fish.

4 (6-ounce) yellowfin tuna fillets

1⅓ cups Olive Oil Mayonnaise (page 240) or regular mayonnaise

¼ cup chopped red onion, plus thin slices for serving

¼ cup chopped fresh flat-leaf parsley leaves

Freshly squeezed juice of 1 lemon

2 tablespoons brined capers, drained

Salt and freshly ground black pepper

4 challah rolls, homemade (page 200) or purchased, or 8 slices Country White Bread, homemade (page 203) or purchased, toasted

1 Set a large, covered steamer basket over an inch of simmering water. Add the tuna and cover the pot. Steam until the tuna is just cooked through (it should still be faintly pink in the center), about 10 minutes. Cool, then flake into bite-size pieces.

2 In a medium bowl, combine the tuna, mayonnaise, chopped onion, parsley, lemon juice, and capers. Season with salt and pepper. Fill the rolls with the salad and top with onion slices before sandwiching.

DUCK CLUB SANDWICH

MAKES 4 SANDWICHES

Using succulent duck breast elevates the humble turkey club to a more regal level. Add the sweetness of raisin bread, the crispiness of bacon, and a dollop of creamy mayo to bring it all together and you've got a club sandwich that will put all others to shame. We serve it with sweet potato chips in the restaurant, for a homey touch.

4 (8-ounce) Muscovy duck breasts

Perfect Roast Seasoning (page 251) or kosher salt and freshly ground black pepper

½ cup Olive Oil Mayonnaise (page 240) or regular mayonnaise

12 slices Raisin Walnut Bread (page 202) or other raisin bread, toasted

4 tablespoons crumbled cooked bacon (from 4 slices)

2 cups shredded iceberg lettuce

2 small tomatoes, thinly sliced

1 small red onion, thinly sliced

1 Preheat the oven to 400°F.

2 Using a sharp knife, score the fat of the duck breasts, taking care not to cut through to the meat. Season the duck generously. Heat a large skillet over medium-high heat until very hot. Sear the duck breasts, skin side down, until the skin browns and fat is rendered, about 8 minutes. Transfer the duck, skin side up, to a rimmed baking sheet. Roast until a thermometer inserted into the thickest part of the duck registers 140°F (the duck will continue to cook as it cools), about 15 minutes. Remove from the oven. Once cool, slice very thin against the grain.

3 To assemble the sandwich, spread 1 tablespoon mayonnaise on each of 4 slices of toast and sprinkle with half of the bacon. Divide the lettuce evenly among the bread slices, and top each with half of the duck slices. Top with a second layer of toast. Spread the remaining mayonnaise over the slices. Sprinkle with the remaining bacon. Top with tomato slices, red onion, and the remaining duck. Cover the sandwiches with the remaining slices of toast, cut into quarters, and serve.

GRILLED STEAK SANDWICH
WITH HORSERADISH CREAM

MAKES 4 SANDWICHES

Most people make steak sandwiches with leftover meat. Not us. We start with shell steaks that we grill up rare and juicy specifically for this sandwich. Then we layer the sliced meat with homemade horseradish cream, pickles, and crunchy iceberg lettuce. It's straightforward, classic, and supremely satisfying.

HORSERADISH CREAM

½ cup sour cream

1 tablespoon drained prepared horseradish

¼ teaspoon freshly squeezed lemon juice

¼ teaspoon salt

⅛ teaspoon freshly ground black pepper

STEAK

4 (7-ounce) shell steaks

4 teaspoons garlic oil (see page 235) or extra-virgin olive oil, plus more for drizzling

Perfect Sauté Seasoning (page 251) or salt and freshly ground white or black pepper

4 (5-ounce) ciabatta rolls, halved horizontally

1 cup shredded iceberg lettuce

1 cup very thinly sliced Garlic Dill Pickle (page 228)

1 TO MAKE THE HORSERADISH CREAM: Combine the sour cream, horseradish, lemon juice, salt, and pepper in a bowl. Cover with plastic wrap and chill until ready to use.

2 TO MAKE THE STEAKS: Preheat a grill pan or other heavy skillet until very hot, about 5 minutes. Brush the steaks with the oil and season generously. Grill the steaks to the desired doneness, about 2 minutes per side for medium-rare. Let the steaks stand for 5 minutes before thinly slicing against the grain.

3 Drizzle the bread with oil and season lightly. Grill the bread until crisp and golden, 1 to 2 minutes per side.

4 Spread the bread with the horseradish cream. Fill the sandwiches with steak slices, lettuce, and pickle. Serve hot.

BARBECUED PORK SANDWICH

We are fortunate to have a huge Ecuadorean contingency working in our restaurants. It all started with our friend Francisco Palaquibay, who has worked with us since 1989, when Eric was the chef at Nick and Eddie's in SoHo. When we opened Blue Ribbon Bakery with its enormous oven, Francisco and his fellow countrymen would often ask to use it to roast whole pigs to take to parties. This went on for a little while before we said, "Hey, guys—when are you going to roast a pig for us?" Finally, we brought in a few pork shoulders and the guys did an Ecuadorean-style rub with garlic, cumin, and vegetables and served it up at our staff meal. The second that aromatic pork came out of the oven, we all just pounced on it. Eventually we were able to hold ourselves back long enough to put the meat on buns, then somebody got the idea to add a little of our great barbecue sauce, and this sandwich was born.

16 garlic cloves, peeled

2 small yellow onions, roughly chopped

1 large carrot, peeled and chopped

1 large celery stalk, chopped

3 tablespoons ground cumin

¼ cup kosher salt

5 pounds pork butt

4 cups Barbecue Sauce (page 243)

Shredded iceberg lettuce, for serving

6 to 8 ciabatta rolls, halved horizontally, soft centers pulled out, toasted, for serving

Garlic Dill Pickles (page 228), for serving

Coleslaw (page 233), for serving

1 Combine the garlic, onions, carrot, celery, cumin, and salt in a food processor. Puree until smooth, adding ½ cup water at the end to finish smoothing out the marinade. Place the pork in a large, deep roasting pan. Rub the pork generously with the marinade; cover and refrigerate for at least 2 hours or overnight.

2 When you are ready to cook the pork, preheat the oven to 350°F.

3 Add water to the baking pan so that it comes halfway up the sides of the pork. Cover the pan tightly with aluminum foil and transfer to the oven. Bake until the pork is very tender and falling apart, about 5 hours. Check the pan occasionally to make sure that the water has not evaporated; add a little more water if necessary.

recipe continues

4   Remove from the oven. Let the pork stand until cool enough to handle. The pork will keep, covered, in the refrigerator for up to 5 days.

5   Increase the oven temperature to 400°F.

6   Shred the pork with a fork or pull apart with your fingers, discarding any excess fat. Combine the meat with 3 cups of the sauce in a large baking dish. Heat the pork mixture in the oven until bubbly, 5 to 10 minutes.

7   Divide the pork and shredded lettuce among the ciabatta rolls. Serve, with the remaining 1 cup sauce, the pickles, and the coleslaw on the side.

BLT ON WHOLE-WHEAT TOAST

MAKES 4 SANDWICHES

P art of what we try to do at Blue Ribbon is to perfect the ordinary diner food that we grew up on. Sometimes it involves reworking entire recipes, like with our Duck Club Sandwich (page 216). But sometimes, it's just a matter of using the very best ingredients and treating them carefully. Such is the case with this BLT; it's the best of its kind without any fancy add-ins. The only trick is to cut the bacon into bite-size pieces so you don't end up pulling the sandwich apart on your first bite.

8 slices whole-wheat bread, toasted

¼ cup mayonnaise, homemade (page 240) or purchased

16 slices cooked bacon, cut into 1-inch pieces

3 small tomatoes, thinly sliced

1 cup chopped romaine lettuce leaves

Garlic Dill Pickle (page 228), for serving (optional)

Spread each slice of bread with mayonnaise. Layer the bacon, tomatoes, and lettuce on 4 of the slices of bread. Top with the remaining bread. Serve with pickles if you like.

THE BLUE REUBEN SANDWICH

This is another Blue Ribbon mainstay with its roots firmly in Jersey, on Route 3 to be exact. We first tasted a Reuben (the corned beef, cheese, and sauerkraut sandwich) at the Tick Tock Diner and it was a revelation—the idea that a grilled sandwich could be more than just a grilled cheese! When we opened Blue Ribbon bakery, we intended to do a grilled chorizo and cheese sandwich, playing off our fantastic memories of dipping bread into spicy chorizo oil at tapas bars in Spain. We planned to call it the C & C Sandwich, for chorizo and cheddar. Somewhere along the way we stuffed some coleslaw in the bread, and it reminded us of the sauerkraut in a Reuben. Of course, it then presented us with an opportunity for a little menu humor by calling it the Blue Reuben. When it comes to puns, we're easy to please.

4 (5-ounce) sandwich baguettes, cut in half horizontally

10 ounces Spanish chorizo, thinly sliced

6 ounces good-quality cheddar cheese, sliced

1 cup Coleslaw (page 233)

Red Wine Sauce (page 236), for serving (optional)

1   Preheat the oven to 400°F.

2   Place the baguette halves, cut side up, on a baking sheet. Cover the bottom halves with the chorizo slices and top with half of the cheese slices. Place a layer of coleslaw evenly on the top halves and cover it with the remaining cheese.

3   Transfer the baking sheet to the oven and bake until the cheese is melted and bubbling, 5 to 7 minutes. Press the sandwich halves together. Cut in half on the diagonal and serve hot, with red wine sauce, for dipping, if desired.

building blocks

▣ garlic dill pickles ▣ roasted tomatoes ▣ roasted red peppers

▣ grilled red onions ▣ pickled peppers ▣ coleslaw

▣ fennel slaw ▣ roasted garlic puree and garlic oil ▣ shallot

confit ▣ red wine sauce ▣ mustard sauce ▣ hollandaise sauce

▣ olive oil mayonnaise ▣ anchovy paste ▣ blue ribbon hot

sauce ▣ barbecue sauce ▣ house vinaigrette ▣ herb butter ▣

garlic butter ▣ spicy chicken sausage ▣ chicken stock ▣ veal

stock ▣ chicken gravy ▣ perfect roast seasoning ▣ perfect

sauté seasoning ▣ fried chicken seasoning

This chapter is really what it's all about. Sauces, stocks, condiments, and the like that are made in your own kitchen, rather than the ones that come out of plastic bottles with brightly colored labels, are what will define your home cooking. The funny thing is, in our culinary school experience, we've seen that many professional chefs are reluctant to learn to make these basics. We watched many of our classmates hem and haw at the thought of yet another day of stock making, or another recipe that used the same old (i.e., "classic") recipe for Red Wine Sauce (page 236); but we have always reveled in the repetition and welcomed any opportunity to further our understanding of the basics. Too many cooks these days just want to learn fancy plate decoration or try their luck at combining random ingredients. But without the solid understanding of how to make the simple sublime (an understanding best developed with sauce making), it's all just a shot in the dark. Don't be scared of stocks or sauces; they make cooking fun.

For some at-home cooks, it may be easier to think of these recipes as "condiments." We use our Olive Oil Mayonnaise (page 240) and all its variations for so much more than sandwich spreads; they work as salad dressings, dips, and even glazes for meat and fish. Barbecue Sauce (page 243) makes an excellent glaze for roasted meat, but it also works beautifully with shrimp. Coleslaw (page 233) and Fennel Slaw (page 234) are terrific as easy side dishes or toppings for sandwiches; it just depends if you want to serve them inside or alongside the bun. Making Chicken Stock (page 247) and Veal Stock (page 248) takes a little more time than going to the corner shop to buy it in a can or box, but in terms of effort we think they're about equal. And the leap in quality the home-made stocks will impart to all your recipes is indescribably huge. Same with Garlic Dill Pickles (page 228); they're delicious and loads of fun to make. You may feel like a mad scientist stirring your fragrant brew, but that's probably one of the things we love the most about cooking.

GARLIC DILL PICKLES

MAKES ABOUT 18 PICKLES

There's a great deli in Jersey called Tabatchnick's, and when we were little kids our dad used to give us a pickle to keep us quiet while he shopped. That's why we always insisted on accompanying him on deli runs—we would just hop out of the car and race to that pickle barrel. Eric would get the garlic dill and Bruce would go for the half-sour. Then, when we got a little older, we started making our own pickles. We got hold of a book from the gardening supply company Ortho called *All About Pickling*, and we used it as a road map. We took over our dad's garden and pickled everything we grew.

This recipe will give you a very classic, garlicky dill pickle. If you like half-sours, eat the pickles while they are still bright green, at about 3 days. Sour-pickle fans should let theirs marinate for at least another day or two.

2 pounds Kirby cucumbers, scrubbed

2 tablespoons white vinegar

¼ cup kosher salt

2 tablespoons sliced garlic

2 tablespoons chopped fresh dill

1 tablespoon brown or yellow mustard seeds

1 bay leaf

1 Chill the cucumbers in a bowl of ice for at least 30 minutes and up to overnight in the refrigerator.

2 In a medium nonreactive pot over medium-high heat, combine 4 cups water, the vinegar, and the salt and bring to a boil. Cook, stirring occasionally, until the salt has dissolved, 3 to 5 minutes. Take the pot off the heat and allow the mixture to cool to room temperature.

3 Drain the cucumbers and place in a large bowl. Add the garlic, dill, mustard seeds, and bay leaf. Pour the water mixture over the cucumbers. Place a plate or other weight on top of the cucumbers so they are completely submerged in the liquid; if necessary add more cold water to cover. Cover the bowl tightly with plastic wrap and let it stand at room temperature for 3 to 4 days. Transfer to the refrigerator for up to 1 week.

ROASTED TOMATOES

MAKES 2 CUPS

Roasted tomatoes are so nice to have around. They taste sweeter, earthier than fresh ones, with a profound flavor that still adds good acidity to a dish. They're really great for the wintertime, or whenever you can't get good tomatoes at the market

16 cherry or grape tomatoes, halved lengthwise

5 to 7 tablespoons extra-virgin olive oil, as needed

Perfect Roast Seasoning (page 250), or kosher salt and freshly ground black pepper

1 Preheat the oven to 225°F.

2 Arrange the tomatoes cut side up on a rimmed baking sheet. Drizzle with 1 tablespoon of the oil and sprinkle with seasoning. Roast until the tomatoes are shriveled and much of their juices have condensed but the tomatoes are not dry, 1 to 1½ hours. Let cool, transfer to an airtight container, cover with a film of olive oil, and refrigerate for up to 2 weeks.

blue ribbon wisdom

ROASTED TOMATO TIPS

- A mix of red and yellow tomatoes looks great in any dish.
- Substitute 4 to 6 plum tomatoes if they look better than the cherry or grape tomatoes at the market. Roast them for 1½ to 2 hours.
- You can scatter rosemary or thyme branches in the pan along with the tomatoes as they roast to add a nice herby flavor.

ROASTED RED PEPPERS

When roasted, red peppers become velvety smooth and their sweetness mellows into something luscious and rich, especially when glossed with plenty of good olive oil. We use them for sandwiches, in salads, and to flavor mayo or even hummus. Make extra and you'll find yourself tossing them in just about every dish you make. The peppers will keep in the refrigerator, covered, for up to 3 weeks.

2 red bell peppers

ON THE STOVETOP

1   Rinse the peppers with water and pat dry with a paper towel.

2   Turn on the gas stove burner to medium-high and, using kitchen tongs, place the pepper on the grate. When the pepper is blackened on one side, about 2 minutes, use the tongs to flip the pepper to the other side.

3   When the pepper is completely blackened, place it in a bowl and cover with a lid or plastic wrap. Repeat the process with the remaining pepper.

4   Allow the peppers to sit, covered, in the bowl for 20 minutes. Then use a paper towel to scrape off the skins. Slice the peppers into strips and scrape out the cores and seeds.

IN THE OVEN

1   Preheat the broiler. Rinse the peppers with water and pat dry with a paper towel.

2   Cut the tops off the peppers and then cut them in half. Scrape out the cores and seeds. Lay the pepper halves as flat as possible on a rimmed baking sheet, skin side up. Broil the peppers until blistered, about 5 minutes.

3   Once the peppers are cool enough to handle, use a paper towel to scrape off the skins. Slice the peppers into strips.

GRILLED RED ONIONS

MAKES ABOUT 1 CUP

We love grilled onions, but if you don't want to bother firing up the grill, you can also broil them. It's a quicker way of cooking them and is a good option if you want to do a lot at once. They're terrific to have around, so we recommend you get in the habit of making them on a regular basis. Every time you turn the broiler on, even if it's just to heat up pizza for the kids, put in a tray of onions. That way you'll always have them on hand for sandwiches, salads, sauces, or whatever.

2 red onions	1 tablespoon extra-virgin olive oil

1 Preheat the broiler.

2 Roughly chop the onions and toss with the olive oil. Spread the onions onto a rimmed baking sheet and broil until golden brown, about 5 minutes. The onions will keep in the refrigerator, covered, for up to 3 weeks.

PICKLED PEPPERS

MAKES ABOUT 1 PINT

As all sandwich lovers know, these are a superb condiment. Add them to your cold cuts once and you'll never want to make a sandwich without them. And as all spicy snack lovers know, they are great all on their own, eaten right out of the jar.

2 whole jalapeño peppers	1 whole long red chile pepper
2 whole serrano peppers	White vinegar, for covering

1 Bring a small saucepan of water to a boil. Add the whole jalapeños, serranos, and red chile pepper; cook for 1 minute. Drain.

2 Place the peppers in a small airtight container. Pour white vinegar over the peppers to cover. Seal the container tightly and refrigerate for 3 days before slicing and using. The peppers will keep in the refrigerator for at least 1 month.

COLESLAW

There's nothing more traditional in world cuisine than pickled cabbage; whether they call it kimchi, sauerkraut, or what have you, everybody's got their own version of coleslaw. This is truly everybody's favorite side dish. It's a great side salad, with an unbelievable crunch, and we like to think it just evokes happiness.

½ head of white cabbage, shredded

¼ cup grated carrot

1 tablespoon chopped fresh flat-leaf parsley leaves

1 tablespoon caraway seeds

¼ small yellow onion, roughly chopped

¼ cup white vinegar

1 tablespoon mayonnaise, homemade (page 240) or purchased

1½ teaspoons kosher salt

1½ teaspoons sugar

¾ teaspoon freshly ground black pepper

½ cup canola oil

1   In a large bowl, toss together the cabbage, carrot, parsley, and caraway seeds.

2   In the bowl of a food processor fitted with the blade attachment, pulse together the onion, vinegar, mayonnaise, salt, sugar, and pepper until combined. With the motor running, slowly drizzle in the canola oil until fully combined.

3   Scrape the vinaigrette into the cabbage mixture and toss well. Cover the coleslaw tightly with plastic wrap and refrigerate for at least 1 hour or up to 3 days before serving.

FENNEL SLAW

This is a take on coleslaw that we put together as a condiment for smoked fish. Fennel has a less assertive flavor than cabbage and works nicely with any type of fish.

1 shallot, peeled and thinly sliced

2 tablespoons dry white wine

2 teaspoons Dijon mustard

1 teaspoon red wine vinegar

½ teaspoon kosher salt, or more to taste

Freshly ground black pepper

3 tablespoons canola oil

1 tablespoon extra-virgin olive oil

1 large carrot, peeled and grated (about 1 cup)

1 fennel bulb, quartered, cored, and thinly sliced lengthwise

½ cup roughly chopped fresh fennel fronds

1 In a small bowl, combine the shallot and wine; let stand for 20 minutes.

2 In a medium bowl, whisk together the mustard, vinegar, salt, and a few grinds of pepper. Slowly whisk in the oils. Stir in the shallot and wine. Taste and adjust the seasoning, if necessary.

3 In a large bowl, combine the carrot, fennel, and fennel fronds. Pour enough vinaigrette over the slaw to coat the vegetables and toss well to combine. Cover tightly with plastic wrap and refrigerate for at least 1 hour or up to 3 days before serving.

ROASTED GARLIC PUREE AND GARLIC OIL

This is super-simple and just about impossible to mess up. Both garlic puree and garlic oil are those building blocks that can be added to so many dishes—to enhance fish, meat, veggies, anything. Anywhere garlic would go, we argue that roasted garlic will get you there.

1 cup whole garlic cloves (from about 3 heads), peeled

1 cup extra-virgin olive oil

1 Preheat the oven to 250°F. Combine the garlic and oil in a baking dish (the oil should cover the garlic). Roast, uncovered, until the garlic is golden and completely softened, about 1½ hours.

2 Cool the garlic slightly. Strain the oil and save for another use. Transfer the garlic cloves to a food processor or blender and process until smooth. Scrape into an airtight container and refrigerate for up to 2 weeks.

SHALLOT CONFIT

MAKES ABOUT 1½ CUPS

Once you get used to having sweet, caramelized shallot confit on hand, you'll add it to almost anything. It will liven up any sauce or salad, it can be used as a condiment on grilled meats or fish, and it's terrific in sandwiches or on a cheese plate.

10 small shallots, peeled

1 cup extra-virgin olive oil

1 Preheat the oven to 325°F.

2 Combine the shallots and oil in a small ovenproof dish; cover with foil. Bake until the shallots are light golden and completely softened, about 1½ hours. Cool to room temperature. The shallots will last up to 3 weeks in an airtight container in the refrigerator.

RED WINE SAUCE

MAKES 1½ CUPS

This traditional French sauce uses a combination of red wine and port, which gives it an especially deep, intense flavor and satiny texture. And you can even make it ahead (see Blue Ribbon Wisdom opposite).

6½ tablespoons unsalted butter, cold and cut into pieces

2 large shallots, finely chopped

2 cups dry red wine

⅔ cup port or other fortified wine

4 sprigs of fresh thyme

1 cup Veal Stock (page 248)

Kosher salt and freshly ground black pepper

1 In a medium skillet, melt 1½ tablespoons of the butter over medium-high heat. Add the shallots and cook, stirring, until translucent, about 3 minutes.

2 Add the wine, port, and thyme. Bring to a boil, then reduce the heat so the mixture simmers. Cook until the liquid has reduced by half, about 20 minutes.

3 Add the stock, and simmer until the mixture has reduced by half again, 10 to 15 minutes more; strain and return the mixture to the heat.

4 Whisk in the remaining 5 tablespoons butter, a little bit at a time, until fully incorporated. Season with salt and pepper. Cover and keep warm.

NOTE Although a whisk works well for emulsifying the butter into the sauce, for a stronger emulsion, we like to use an immersion blender.

blue ribbon wisdom

FAST RED WINE SAUCE Whenever you have red wine left over, put it in a pot with some onions or shallots and reduce it by three fourths. Then just keep it in the fridge until you need it. Add a few tablespoons to boost the flavor of pan sauces, soups, stews, or almost anything you're cooking.

MAKE IT AHEAD OR MAKE IT THAT DAY You can make the red wine sauce up to a month ahead. Make the sauce up to the point of adding the butter (through step 3), and freeze it; you can even freeze it in ice cube trays, so you'll have single-serving portions of the sauce ready to go. When you're ready to use it, just defrost in the refrigerator, bring it to a simmer, and whisk in the butter.

You can also make it the day you need it. If you'll be serving it for dinner, you can whip it up in the morning and keep it warm (150°F to 160°F). It should last for up to 6 hours. But if it does break for some reason, not to worry. Bring the sauce to a boil, drop in an ice cube, and use an immersion blender to bring it back into shape.

MUSTARD SAUCE

MAKES ABOUT 1½ CUPS

This sharp and savory mustard sauce makes a great sandwich spread, dipping sauce, or salad dressing.

½ teaspoon red wine vinegar

½ teaspoon freshly squeezed lemon juice

Pinch of kosher salt

1 large egg yolk

2½ tablespoons whole-grain mustard

2 teaspoons Dijon mustard

½ teaspoon finely chopped shallot

1 cup extra-virgin olive oil

1½ tablespoons sour cream

1 In a medium bowl, whisk together the vinegar, lemon juice, and salt until the salt dissolves. Whisk in the egg, mustards, and shallot until the mixture is well blended and pale yellow.

2 Whisking constantly, very slowly drizzle in the oil until the mixture is fully combined. Whisk in the sour cream. Transfer the sauce to an airtight container and refrigerate for up to 1 week.

HOLLANDAISE SAUCE

A wire whisk beats a steady stream of shimmering melted butter and golden egg yolks to a fluffy consistency that is so pure and refined that it looks like thousands of tiny diamonds. It sounds like magic, and as we used to watch our dad prepare his famous eggs Benedict we were mesmerized. This wondrous concoction of yolks and clarified butter is one of the most loved and revered sauces in the culinary world. It is brilliant with steak, eggs, french fries, roasted asparagus, and just about anything else that can be dipped or dunked. Hollandaise is also a great base for other flavors; just add some caviar, roasted garlic puree, or a touch of roasted tomato to really mix things up. So it's not surprising that hollandaise is one of our favorite things to cook and definitely one of our favorite things to eat.

1 cup (2 sticks) unsalted butter

5 large egg yolks

1 teaspoon dry white wine

¾ teaspoon freshly squeezed lemon juice

¼ teaspoon kosher salt, plus more to taste

Small pinch of cayenne

Freshly ground white pepper

TRADITIONAL METHOD

1 Melt the butter in a small saucepan until frothy. Spoon off the foam. Cover and keep warm.

2 Bring a medium saucepan filled with 2 inches of water to a simmer. In a large, heat-proof bowl set over the simmering water, whisk together the egg yolks, wine, lemon juice, salt, cayenne, and white pepper. Whisk in a figure-eight motion. As the mixture begins to thicken, switch to a circular motion (this will make it more stable). Alternate between figure-eight and circular whisking, until the mixture is glossy and holds a peak. If the mixture begins to steam, whisk it off the heat for several seconds to cool slightly.

3 Remove the egg mixture from the heat. Slowly whisk in the clear golden butter, leaving the milk solids at the bottom of the saucepan. Serve immediately, or remove from the heat, cover tightly, and keep warm over the pot of hot water (off the heat) for up to 30 minutes.

BLENDER METHOD

1 Melt the butter in a medium saucepan until frothy. Spoon off the foam.

2 In the blender, combine the wine, lemon juice, salt, cayenne, and white pepper. Add the egg yolks and blend for 3 to 5 seconds until thickened.

3 With the blender running, slowly pour in the hot butter, leaving the milk solids at the bottom of the pan. Spoon the sauce into a bowl. (Before serving, reheat in a bowl set over a pot of simmering water, if necessary.)

blue ribbon wisdom

BROKEN SAUCE Hollandaise will keep only as long as you keep the temperature within the 140°F to 150°F range. If it falls much below that it can break, and if it goes much higher than that it will break. This is not a sauce you can put in the fridge and take out when you want it. It really needs to be made within an hour or so of serving. Now, if something unexpected happens and the sauce separates, all is not lost. There are a couple tricks to bring it together again. If it has become too cold, add boiling water tablespoon by tablespoon and stir. Or, take ¼ cup of the broken hollandaise and put it into a clean mixing bowl and add a tablespoon of hot water; stir until the sauce emulsifies and then slowly whisk the rest of the broken sauce into your new sauce. If the sauce gets too hot, you can go through the same process using ice water.

VARIATIONS ▣ As long as the ingredient you're adding is the same temperature as the hollandaise, there's no limit to the flavorings. Here are some favorites:

Anchovy paste, homemade (page 241) or purchased

Roasted Tomatoes (page 230)

Salmon roe or black caviar

Pureed green peppercorns (for a fast béarnaise)

Roasted Garlic Puree (page 235)

OLIVE OIL MAYONNAISE

The conventional wisdom we picked up in France is that a chef should never use olive oil when making mayonnaise, that the flavors are too assertive and will overpower whatever dish that sauce accompanies. It took a few years, but we finally worked that dogma out of our system. The fact of the matter is that mayonnaise, that great building block of American cuisine, gets even better when made with olive oil. And using olive oil allows us to avoid polyunsaturated fats as well as peanut oil, which is a tricky ingredient with our allergen-conscious patrons.

1½ teaspoons red wine vinegar	2 teaspoons Dijon mustard
¼ teaspoon kosher salt	¾ cup canola oil
1 large egg	½ cup extra-virgin olive oil
1 large egg yolk	Freshly ground black pepper

In a large bowl, whisk together the vinegar and salt until the salt dissolves. Whisk in the egg, egg yolk, and mustard until fully combined. Whisking constantly and vigorously, very slowly drizzle in the oils until the mixture is fully emulsified and thickened. Season with pepper to taste.

VARIATION ◙ SWEET ONION MAYONNAISE

In a blender or food processor, puree ½ cup Grilled Red Onions (page 232). Pulse in ½ cup Olive Oil Mayonnaise until well combined. Store in an airtight container in the refrigerator for up to 1 week. Makes about 1 cup.

VARIATION ◙ ROASTED TOMATO MAYONNAISE

In a blender or food processor, puree 1 cup Roasted Tomatoes (page 230) until smooth (about ½ cup puree). Push the puree through a mesh strainer; use a plastic spatula to press on the puree. Discard the solids. Stir 1 cup Olive Oil Mayonnaise into the tomato mixture. Cover tightly with plastic wrap and chill until ready to use. Store in an airtight container in the refrigerator for up to 1 week. Makes about 2 cups.

In a blender or food processor, puree 1 cup Shallot Confit (page 235). Pulse in 1 cup Olive Oil Mayonnaise until well combined. Store in an airtight container in the refrigerator for up to 1 week. Makes about 2 cups.

Fold ¾ cup Olive Oil Mayonnaise, 3 tablespoons Mexican honey (see page 27), 1 tablespoon whole-grain mustard, and 1 tablespoon Dijon mustard together. Store in an airtight container in the refrigerator for up to 1 week. Makes about 1 cup.

ANCHOVY PASTE

MAKES ABOUT 1 CUP

So you hate anchovies? Well, so did we until we mixed them with olive oil, briny capers, and zesty lemon juice. Honestly, this may be the best thing we have ever made. Slather it on a grilled steak or roasted fish, marinated veggies, or even crusty toast topped with grilled onions. The possibilities are endless, and you can now make use of that tin of anchovies that has been sitting forlorn on some dark high shelf in your cupboard. Bonus!

6 tablespoons drained anchovies	½ cup extra-virgin olive oil
2 tablespoons drained capers	¾ teaspoon freshly squeezed lemon juice
1 garlic clove, finely chopped	

Using a food processor, puree together the anchovies, capers, and garlic. Slowly drizzle in the oil, pureeing until a smooth paste is achieved. Drizzle in the lemon juice and puree until smooth.

BLUE RIBBON HOT SAUCE

MAKES 4 CUPS

When we opened Blue Ribbon Brooklyn with a much larger kitchen than we have in SoHo, we decided that we wanted to make everything we could from scratch—including all the ice creams and many of the condiments, like ketchup, pickles, even our own hot sauce and steak sauce. Well, after a lot of playing around, we realized that A1 was still better than any steak sauce we could make, Ciao Bella made superior vanilla ice cream, and Heinz had us beat on ketchup. But our partner and chef Mike Paritsky did manage to come up with excellent recipes for pickles (see page 228) and this killer hot sauce, which we think is better than anything you can buy. Our secret is the carrots, which make the bright-orange sauce just glow in its bottle. Carrots also add body and sweetness to temper the heat of the habanero chiles. Store the sauce in your refrigerator. It will last for years.

3 cups distilled white vinegar	2 tablespoons salt
3 to 4 red, orange, or yellow habanero chiles, to taste, trimmed and sliced	1 pound carrots, trimmed, peeled, and roughly chopped

1 Combine the vinegar, chiles, and salt in a large nonreactive pot over medium-high heat. Bring to a boil. Let the mixture cool, then puree in a blender and strain.

2 While the peppers are cooking, in a separate pot combine the carrots with water to cover. Simmer until very tender but not overcooked, about 10 minutes. Drain well. Puree the carrots in the blender until smooth (you do not need to strain them), then stir into the strained vinegar mixture. If it's too spicy-hot, thin it down with a little water.

3 Use immediately, or transfer the hot sauce to airtight, sterile jars or bottles and refrigerate.

blue ribbon wisdom

CHOOSING AND USING HABANEROS We always look for solidly red, yellow, and orange habaneros for this recipe. Using partially green chiles will muddy the bright color of the sauce. Also, the red, orange, and yellow chiles are riper and more mature and have a sweeter flavor than the grassy-tasting green ones.

If you've ever chopped a couple of chile peppers, then rubbed your eye, you know the pain chile fingers can inflict. Always wash your hands with lots of hot, soapy water when you're finished handling chiles. Same goes for your knife and chopping board.

BARBECUE SAUCE

MAKES ABOUT 4 CUPS

This is the sauce we make especially for our Barbecued Pork Sandwich (page 219) and for the spareribs in the Pupu Platter (page 56), but it really makes a terrific, slightly sweet and tangy glaze for just about any grilled or broiled meat.

3 cups ketchup

1 cup pure maple syrup

¾ cup light beer, such as a pale ale

½ cup honey

¼ cup cola

2 teaspoons Blue Ribbon Hot Sauce (page 242) or other hot sauce, plus more to taste

1 teaspoon cayenne pepper

1 serrano chile, seeded if desired, chopped

1 In a heavy nonreactive saucepan over medium-high heat, stir together the ketchup, maple syrup, beer, honey, cola, hot sauce, cayenne pepper, and serrano chile and bring to a boil. Reduce the heat to medium-low and simmer, uncovered, until the mixture has reduced to 4 cups, about 1½ hours. Stir occasionally so that the mixture does not burn.

2 Strain the sauce through a medium-fine mesh sieve. If not using right away, let cool, cover, and refrigerate until ready to use, up to a few months.

HOUSE VINAIGRETTE

MAKES ABOUT 2 CUPS

This dressing has a delicate herb flavor, balanced with a little kick from the Dijon mustard and red wine vinegar.

¼ cup red wine vinegar

¼ teaspoon kosher salt

Small pinch of dried oregano

Small pinch of dried thyme

1 tablespoon Dijon mustard

1⅓ cups extra-virgin olive oil

Freshly ground black pepper

In a bowl, whisk together the vinegar, salt, oregano, and thyme until the salt dissolves. Whisk in the mustard. Whisking constantly, slowly drizzle in the oil until fully incorporated. Season with pepper to taste. The vinaigrette will keep in the refrigerator, covered, for up to 1 month.

HERB BUTTER

MAKES A GENEROUS ½ CUP

Butter is one of our favorite ingredients to experiment with. This one is like a spreadable herb garden.

8 tablespoons (1 stick) unsalted butter, softened

4 teaspoons chopped fresh flat-leaf parsley leaves

2 teaspoons chopped fresh fennel fronds

2 teaspoons chopped fresh chives

2 pinches of kosher salt

2 pinches of freshly ground black pepper

In a medium bowl, mix the butter, parsley, fennel fronds, chives, salt, and pepper. Refrigerate, covered, until needed. The butter will keep in an airtight container for 2 weeks in the fridge and 3 months in the freezer.

GARLIC BUTTER

MAKES ABOUT ¾ CUP

We fondly refer to this as "magic butter." It makes all good things even better. Make up a batch of it and keep it in the fridge or freezer. You can use it to cook clams or mussels; just combine it with a little white wine in the pot with the shellfish, cover, steam, and you don't need anything else. You can add it to pasta to make a great sauce, or make shrimp scampi with it. Try combining it with chopped tomatoes and anchovies for a great bruschetta, or use it to top grilled steak, steamed green beans, or corn on the cob. It goes with basically any dish there is. Magic.

8 tablespoons (1 stick) unsalted butter, softened

1½ teaspoons finely chopped garlic

1½ teaspoons finely chopped fresh flat-leaf parsley leaves

½ teaspoon finely chopped fresh rosemary

½ teaspoon finely chopped fresh thyme leaves

⅛ teaspoon kosher salt

⅛ teaspoon freshly ground black pepper

Combine the butter, garlic, parsley, rosemary, thyme, salt, and pepper in a bowl; mix well. Cover and refrigerate until ready to use. Garlic butter will keep, refrigerated in a covered container, for up to 2 weeks. Or freeze for up to 3 months.

SPICY CHICKEN SAUSAGE

MAKES 4 POUNDS; SERVES 6 TO 8

You know the old saying "nobody likes to see the sausage being made"? Well, the best way to avoid wondering what's in the sausage is to make it yourself. This is our favorite sausage recipe; we use the ground chicken to keep it lean and we don't skimp on the seasoning. This is spiced with our Paella Basquez (page 113) in mind. If you're making these sausages to eat on their own, cut the peppery seasonings in half.

4 pounds ground dark meat chicken (with skin, if possible)

¼ cup chopped garlic

3½ tablespoons kosher salt

3 tablespoons hot paprika

3 tablespoons crushed red pepper flakes

2½ tablespoons whole fennel seeds

1½ tablespoons dried oregano

2 teaspoons coarsely ground black pepper

1 teaspoon cayenne pepper

1 tablespoon extra-virgin olive oil, plus more, if needed, for cooking

1 Using your hands, mix the chicken, garlic, salt, paprika, red pepper flakes, fennel seeds, oregano, black pepper, and cayenne pepper together in a large bowl. Cover and refrigerate for 4 hours or overnight.

2 To cook the sausage, make 1½-inch-thick patties out of the mixture. Heat the oil in a skillet over medium heat. Cook the patties in the oil, turning once, until browned on both sides and cooked through, 3 to 5 minutes per side.

VARIATION ▣ SPICY CHICKEN LINK SAUSAGES

Fill pork casings with the sausage meat, making links 5 to 6 inches long. Transfer the links to a wire rack over a rimmed baking sheet and bake until their internal temperature reaches 125°F, 15 to 20 minutes. Serve hot or allow the sausages to cool to room temperature, then cover and refrigerate until ready to use.

CHICKEN STOCK

We like to take the simplest approach possible to our chicken stock. We use it for so many recipes that we want it to have a clean flavor that will work with anything. We don't add anything our own grandma wouldn't add—just carrots, onions, and aromatics for a little sweetness and body.

5 pounds chicken bones

½ cup kosher salt

2 cups chopped carrots

2 cups chopped onions

2 cups chopped leeks, washed well

5 garlic cloves, peeled

2 tablespoons black peppercorns

1 bay leaf

1 Put the chicken bones in a large bowl and cover them with 1 gallon cold water. Stir in the salt and let the bones soak for 30 minutes.

2 Rinse and drain the bones; transfer them to a large stockpot and cover with 1 gallon of cold water. Bring to a boil over high heat. Skim off the foam as it rises to the top.

3 Reduce the heat to medium and add the carrots, onions, leeks, garlic, black peppercorns, and bay leaf. Simmer for 3 hours.

4 Strain the stock into a bowl. Use immediately, refrigerate for up to 3 days, or freeze for up to 3 months.

blue ribbon wisdom

SKIMMING STOCK The most critical step with stock making can often be overlooked. The key is to put the chicken bones into the cold water and bring it to a boil before anything else is added. Any impurities will rise to the top as foam and will be easy to skim off. If you add the vegetables too soon, they'll get in the way of the foam. You'll constantly have to do battle with them to skim off the impurities, making for a frustrating experience.

VEAL STOCK

Making stock is often seen as a daunting task, especially in the home kitchen. But if you take a basic approach to it (it's just bones and water, people!), the whole process can really be enjoyable. You're creating something useful out of something you might ordinarily just throw away.

5 pounds veal bones

2 cups chopped carrots

2 cups chopped onions

2 cups chopped leeks, washed well

5 garlic cloves, peeled

2 tablespoons black peppercorns

1 bay leaf

1   Preheat the oven to 425°F.

2   Scatter the bones in a large roasting pan and roast until dark golden brown, about 1 hour.

3   Using a slotted spoon, transfer the bones to a large stockpot. Add the carrots, onions, leeks, and garlic to the roasting pan and return to the oven. Roast the vegetables until they are golden brown, about 20 minutes. Using a wooden spoon or spatula, stir the vegetables and scrape any browned bits off the bottom of the pan. Transfer the vegetables to the stockpot.

4   Cover the bones and vegetables with 3 gallons of water. Add the peppercorns and bay leaf. Simmer the stock for 4 hours.

5   Strain the stock into a bowl. Use immediately, refrigerate for up to 3 days, or freeze for up to 3 months.

CHICKEN GRAVY

This is terrific on fried chicken and even better on mashed potatoes.

4 cups chicken bones and wings

2 tablespoons unsalted butter, softened

2 tablespoons all-purpose flour

4 cups chicken stock, homemade (page 247) or purchased

1 tablespoon fresh thyme leaves

½ teaspoon kosher salt, plus more if needed

½ teaspoon freshly ground black pepper, plus more if needed

1 Preheat the oven to 400°F.

2 Spread the chicken bones and wings out on a foil-lined rimmed baking sheet. Roast until well browned, about 1 hour.

3 In a small bowl, combine the softened butter with the flour to make a paste.

4 Transfer the chicken bones and wings, along with any browned bits from the baking sheet, to a large skillet. Pour in the stock and bring to a simmer over medium-high heat. Simmer for 30 minutes. Strain the mixture; discard the bones and wings and return the liquid to the pan over medium-high heat. Stir in the thyme. Whisk in the butter paste, 1 tablespoon at a time, until the sauce is thick and gravy-like. Cook for 1 to 2 minutes more. Season with salt and pepper. Cover and keep warm until needed.

PERFECT ROAST SEASONING

MAKES ABOUT ⅔ CUP

As its name might indicate, this mix is the perfect seasoning for roasted meats. The long cooking time of roasts ensures that the coarse kosher salt is absorbed into the dish, and this mix has just the right proportion of pepper and herb.

¼ cup plus 2 tablespoons kosher salt

3 tablespoons freshly ground black pepper

1½ tablespoons dried thyme

Combine the salt, pepper, and thyme and store in a covered container.

SALT

The reason we came up with our three seasoning mixes is so we can season everything perfectly and quickly in our busy restaurant kitchens.

We use two basic salt varieties at Blue Ribbon: kosher salt and regular table salt. They shouldn't be used interchangeably. Kosher salt has a much coarser grain and, because we measure in volume, we call for twice the amount of the coarser-grained kosher salt than we do for the table salt. Kosher salt is great for roasted meats, bread dough, anything that has a long cooking time, which allows the salt to dissolve into the food and give it a beautifully even seasoning. We use table salt for dishes that have a quick cooking time, like fish or crunchy vegetables, or with lighter baked goods, such as muffins or scones.

Coarse sea salt, such as fleur de sel, is great for sprinkling on steaks right before you serve them. We use it when we're seasoning just for that mouthful, where you want the coarse salt texture and the bright salt flavor.

PERFECT SAUTÉ SEASONING

This is the seasoning mix we use for any dish that has a quick cooking time. The table salt gives an even season; nobody will bite into a crunchy crystal and think there's too much salt. We use the white pepper in this mix so that if we want to make a pan sauce, it gives a smooth and unspeckled appearance.

¼ cup plus 2 tablespoons salt | 1 teaspoon finely ground white pepper

Combine the salt and pepper and store in a covered container.

FRIED CHICKEN SEASONING

This is great to have around to sprinkle over corn on the cob, grilled vegetables, or anywhere you want to add a little heat.

2 teaspoons hot paprika

1½ teaspoons salt

½ teaspoon garlic powder

½ teaspoon onion powder

½ teaspoon dried parsley

½ teaspoon dried basil

¼ teaspoon cayenne pepper

Combine the paprika, salt, garlic powder, onion powder, parsley, basil, and cayenne pepper, and store in a covered container.

SOURCES

AMERICAN STURGEON CAVIAR:
www.911caviar.com

BONITO FLAKES:
www.asianfoodgrocer.com

ESCARGOTS:
www.markys.com

KOMBU:
www.asianfoodgrocer.com

KATAIFI: www.aviglatt.com

MIRIN:
www.asianfoodgrocer.com

PLUM WINE:
www.internet.wines.com

SAKE: www.esake.com

SHISO:
www.asianfoodgrocer.com

SMOKED DUCK BREAST:
www.smokehouse.com

ZATARAIN'S CRAB BOIL:
www.zatarains.com

ACKNOWLEDGMENTS

The recipes and content of this book have been simmering for decades. There are so many who have touched our lives and molded our vision that it would be impossible to thank them all. But let's give it a try. . . .

To our wives, you put up with missed dates, late nights, way too many phone calls, nonexistent weekends, aborted vacations, and in exchange get only half of the attention you deserve. At least you eat well . . . we love you.

Ellen, those pre-baby years were legendary. Countless ninety-hour workweeks, extraordinary pressures, defining what Blue Ribbon would mean for many years to come, and living with two ridiculously obsessive personalities should earn you a medal, but in this case all we can offer is our deep appreciation and unconditional love. Thanks for everything.

Kerry, thanks for keeping us on the straight and narrow, always telling it like it is, and tolerating a little cream and butter in these recipes. Your clarity, motivation, friendship, and, most important, love are paramount to all that we do and all that we aspire to be. Yebo gogo!

Leah, Jason, Brett, and little Tanner. Your smiles, laughs, and honesty make the late nights bearable and the early mornings memorable. We love you!

Dad, your obsession has become ours, you aided and abetted us every step of the way. You sent us to the only school that we ever loved and gave us every tool that we needed to succeed. *Merci, Papa!*

Mom, your soft words and constant reassurance make a chaotic world calm and caring. Thanks for your incredible support and simple yet sublime culinary guidance.

Brother Ken, thanks for making our lives awesome and always having our backs.

Suzanne Allgair, you rule! Partners for life. This book would not exist without all of your dedication and hard work.

Elizabeth Frumin, what more can we say? *We* would not exist without all that you do for us.

Mike Paritsky, Kris Polak, and Sean Santamour—you are Blue Ribbon! You got us here, keep us here, and help get us where we are going. Nothing beats that!

Sefton Stallard, your culinary inspirations seem endless throughout this book, and your friendship endless throughout our lives.

Melissa Clark, who knew this would be so fun (tiring, yes, but fun)? You brought Blue Ribbon to life on each and every page. And all this while you were bringing your own little baby to life as well. Thanks for being a great friend!

Janis Donnaud, without your impetus and direction, this book would still just be another cool idea (and we have plenty of those). But here it is. Thanks for your focus and for keeping us on the right track.

Rica Allannic, our gratitude for your faith in what we do and putting all this together. You and your team at Clarkson Potter really get who we are and where we are coming from, and that's not so evident all the time.

Quentin Bacon, thanks for your great eye and for capturing the essence of what we do. The photos are amazing!

Edward Asfour and Peter Guzy, for your vision and clarity, guidance and friendship. You keep us in line and moving in the right direction. You guys really make what we do a pleasure.

Donna Lachman, thanks for doing what you love to do so that we can do what we love to do. Speechless!

A very special thanks to Mr. Cointreau, Patrick Martin, Patrick Terrien, Chef George, Chef Bernard, and Le Cordon Bleu. Our time under your tutelage was a true education in life. Your continued support is both amazing and humbling.

We would also like to thank: Toshi Ueki, for being an amazing chef and the best partner ever; Big Jimmy, for greeting everybody with a smile and being the face of Blue Ribbon for the last seventeen years; Alex Adams, for missing work on those fateful days; Pizzuli, Favio, Hector, and Felix, for making great food and running the show for all these years; Bowie, for keeping it all in line and striving for excellence; Jose & Fabiola, for amazing breads. Daisy, for standing by us all these years, being an amazing friend to the staff and us, and saying "ciao, darling" each and every day. David Brown, for your unrelenting dedication and making Blue Ribbon home; Dan, Magnus, Berton, Morgan, Jarred, Asa, Sam, Andrew, Johnny, Stan, Shino, Ari, and everyone else who leads the troops into battle each night; Teresa, for always telling it like it is and keeping us in the game; Francisco; for being the patriarch of the most amazing crew; Polanco, wherever you are; Charley, for keeping us cool; Kainen, for chicken burger quality control; Dennis, for helping to pay the rent for all these years (one bottle at a time); Kimball, for just being Kimball; Shalvoy, for keeping the beat; Jen, for artistic inspiration; Rick, for building them and making construction fun; Lobster Man, for eating so many lobsters that we actually call you Lobster Man.

Also: Everyone who has ever run a plate of food up that godforsaken flight of stairs. Everyone who has ever had to suck in their gut just to get a bottle of beer out of the cooler. Everyone who has ever started their shift at 2:30 in the afternoon and who is still looking at a full dining room with an hour wait thirteen hours later. Everyone who ever showed up at 4:00 in the morning to start cleaning up and prepping food for the next day. Everyone who has ever asked "sparkling or flat?" Everyone who ever shucked a thousand oysters in a night. Everyone who ever answered the question "Where do you work?" with "I work at Blue Ribbon." Thank you all from the bottom of our hearts. In the wise words of Frank Zappa, "We are who you is!"

But ultimately we would like to thank each and every person who has ever crossed the threshold at any of the Blue Ribbon restaurants. You are why we do what we do. We love to cook and we exist because you love to eat. Your energy and passion astounds us and inspires us each and every day. You make this restaurant stuff so incredibly fun. Thank you! Thank you! Thank you!

INDEX

Page references in *italics* refer to photographs.